Human Science & Human Dignity

Donald M. MacKay

Foreword by John R. W. Stott

InterVarsity Press
Downers Grove
Illinois 60515

InterVarsity Press is the book-publishing
division of Inter-Varsity Christian
Fellowship, a student movement active on
campus at hundreds of universities, colleges
and schools of nursing. For information
about local and regional activities, write
IVCF, 233 Langdon St.,
Madison, WI 53703.

ISBN 0-87784-461-5
Library of Congress Catalog
Card Number: 79-2383

Printed in the United States of America

Acknowledgments

I am grateful to the following for permission to quote from published works:

George Allen & Unwin, Publishers Ltd. (p. 110)
McGraw-Hill Book Company, New York (pp. 16, 36)
Oxford University Press, Oxford (pp. 36, 37, 42)
Charles Scribners Sons, New York (p. 112)
The Times (pp. 88, 89, 90)
The Tyndale Bulletin (pp. 117, 118)
University Press of America, Washington (pp. 59, 60).

Chapter 5. Mechanism and Meaning

Chapter 6. The Truest Dignity

Foreword

The topic of the 1977 London Lectures in Contemporary Christianity is one of momentous importance: what constitutes authentic 'humanness'? What makes a human being significant? Does modern science undermine human dignity?

I listened to Professor MacKay's lectures with absorbed interest. His keen mind penetrates the heart of every argument, and coolly, dispassionately, he exposes logical fallacies wherever he detects them, in Christians and non-Christians alike.

His courage and compassion impress me as much as his clarity. He dares to welcome the prospect of human engineering in so far as it may diminish human suffering and contribute to truly human welfare. He has such confidence in the God of truth that nothing makes him afraid.

And he is determined to hold fast to the truth in its wholeness. His well-known rejection of reductionism or (as he terms it) 'nothing-buttery' is matched by his resolve to face and to integrate all the available data. Above all, while readily acknowledging that from one point of view a human being is an animal, and from another a mechanism, he refuses to stop there. In order to do full justice to human beings, he introduces us to the concept of a 'hierarchy of levels' at which human life is to be understood and experienced. He is convinced that the highest level of all, in which 'the truest dignity' is to be found, is that of our personal responsibility to our Creator who loves us and invites our responding love. Without this loving relationship human beings are always less than fully human.

The London Lectures Committee are grateful and proud to

have had Donald MacKay as our 1977 lecturer. To come into contact with his Christian mind and heart is to be enriched as a human being.

John R. W. Stott

Preface

As the scientific periscope has come to focus increasingly in our time on man himself, the dignity and meaningfulness of human life seem to many to be threatened as never before. In the name of 'Behaviourism', traditional human categories and values are ridiculed as 'pre-scientific'. Man is analyzed and displayed to popular view as no more than a naked ape, or a programmable biochemical computing machine, or even a complex device for ensuring the proliferation of the particular genes that determined his make-up. Meantime, 'scientific humanists' strive desperately to find a credible basis for human self-respect in a world picture from which God has been banished on the pretended authority of science itself.

Small wonder if for many people today the science of human behaviour is something mankind would be better without, something that smacks of 'Brave New World', subliminal advertising, and the inhuman aloofness of the cynical spectator. Small wonder, perhaps, that in reaction we find today a distressing credulity among sensitive people towards the claims of mystery cults, pseudo-scientific charlatans and the exponents of irrational and undisciplined self-expression. If the rational path of science leads to meaninglessness in the end, what hope is left for mankind save in the dark recesses where the scientist fears or scorns to tread? For those who think on these lines, the defence of human dignity is a rearguard action in which every obstacle to mechanistic understanding is a cherished bastion, and every advance of behavioural science a defeat.

The argument of these lectures is that from the standpoint of biblical Christianity, this whole assessment is radically mistaken. Biblically realistic humanism – a robustly compassionate concern for the fulfilment of our fellow men as God has created them – has nothing to fear from the science of human behaviour. Rather does it demand that we receive thankfully and reckon sensitively with all that can be understood about the complex machinery through which people's personalities are expressed.

Increasing knowledge, however, brings increasing responsibility, including responsibility for any failure to use properly the knowledge we gain. Is the growth of knowledge then always desirable? 'To whom much is given, from him will the more be required'. Is it ever legitimate to 'want not to know'? What principles should guide us in seeking to meet our responsibility honestly and diligently as the science of man advances? How can we prevent education from degenerating into brainwashing, or evangelism into manipulation? And where, in all this, is the focus of significance of what it is to be human? These are questions hotly disputed in our day among both scientists and non-scientists, Christians and non-Christians. My aim in this book is to make a constructive contribution to the debate from a standpoint which unites a concern for the integrity of science with a conviction of the truth of the biblical Christian faith. Although I have mainly Christian readers in mind, I hope that the argument will also be found relevant by anyone who wonders what he would be letting himself in for if he became a Christian. I have been in that position myself.

I am grateful to the Langham Trust for the invitation to deliver the 1977 London Lectures in Contemporary Christianity, on which the book is based. The style of the spoken word has been retained where possible, but I have been greatly helped in the task of revision by my wife and several patient friends. I have particularly valued the steadfast encouragement of my good friend John Stott throughout the planning and execution of the project.

Mrs. Jane Howe and Miss Margaret Hodgson have coped nobly with the tasks of transcription and repeated re-typing.

CHAPTER 1

The Spectator Approach

'And God said, Let us make man in our image, after our likeness; and let them have dominion over the fish of the sea, and over the birds of the air, and over the cattle, and over all the earth. . . .'

In these familiar phrases the Book of Genesis spells out the mysterious dignity of what it means to be human. Encamped in a complex and dangerous world whose every feature, like himself, owes its being to the say-so of his Creator, man is singled out as one who has an explicit task. He is to 'have dominion'. He alone, it would seem, among his fellow creatures, will be held *accountable* for the management – or mismanagement – of the resources at his disposal. For the biblical writers the world is not merely something to be enjoyed or admired – though it is both – but something to be explored and developed by man in a spirit of thankful and responsible stewardship, for the benefit of his fellows and the glory of God. With all his limitations, he has enough likeness to his Creator to be called upon to accept and pursue his Creator's priorities. This – no less – is his destiny and his dignity.

If this sounds like the introduction to a lecture on conservation of the environment, I hope you will not be too disappointed; the point I want to make is a much more general one. For, as it happens, it was on this same biblical foundation that Francis Bacon and the 17th century pioneers of modern science based their hopes of a new and exciting experimental approach to the problem of gathering reliable knowledge. To the early navigators who sought 'dominion over the earth' in a geographical sense, a reliable map could make all the difference between life and death. Why then should not the human community, in the spirit of the same Genesis mandate, send out exploring 'mapmakers' into other dimensions of the physical world? For reliable geographical knowledge you had to take some trouble to put yourself in the way of the evidence, with a minimum of pre-conceived ideas. If then you wanted reliable knowledge in other domains, surely at least as diligent exploratory efforts were called for, with the same humble readiness to be obedient to the data revealed, even where they refused to fit with what men had hitherto thought 'reasonable' or 'commonsense'? In the light of the divine mandate in Genesis, said Bacon, such explorations into nature, in such a spirit, were not merely our right but our duty.

We all know the sequel. The objective method of systematic experimentation, designed to discover what things are like from the standpoint of a detached spectator, has already built up a vastly greater bulk of reliable knowledge than all the efforts of previous ages put together. The roving periscope of the scientist can provide us with an outsider's view of the galaxies at one extreme of size and the depths of the atomic nucleus at the other. It allows us not merely to observe and contemplate, but also to predict, to model, to explain and to exploit the processes it reveals. It affords not only information, but power . . .

And here, of course, is the rub. For among the objects revealed in the scientific mirror, to be dissected, modelled, explained, perchance controlled, it is impossible not to include man himself. In terms of our original metaphor, the triumphant advance of the exploring mapmakers has brought them back to the gates of the camp itself, this time not just to inform the inhabitants, but to inspect them: to make them in their turn the objects of observation. Instruments developed for the exploration of the outside world now find themselves trained upon the camp itself, and ourselves in it, as if we were mere features of that outside world. Admittedly, in field after field the scientific method of viewing-in-detachment has been acclaimed (with some justification) as the antidote to entrenched prejudice and myopia – the only way to 'see things as they really are'. But now that we come to feel the scientific spotlight on the backs of our own necks we are smitten with misgivings. The power to 'see ourselves as ithers see us' may seem as attractive in principle to us as it did to Rabbie Burns; but in practice something seems curiously lacking in the images produced by the scientific mapmakers.

For a start, in nearly all the views offered by their mirror we seem to lose sight of man himself. At one level of analysis, we see only a mass of molecules in wild confusion. At another, we are shown a tangle of self-regulating biochemical mechanisms, controlling such things as the levels of sugar or oxygen in the blood-stream. At yet another, we catch glimpses of a community of millions of microcomputers, each constructed of a network of nerve cells and the whole more complex in its structure than the total pattern of communication links between all the people alive on the earth. From a biological angle, what we see is an organism built on very similar lines to others, using similar components and showing signs (according to some theorists) of similar ancestry. From an ethological angle, we observe an animal whose social behaviour patterns show many resemblances to those of apes, hunting dogs, or humble farmyard fowls. Even in psychological terms, the picture we have is festooned with causal links between entities bearing such outlandish labels as 'drives' or 'contingencies of reinforcement', leaving little or nothing recognizable at first glance as characteristically human. Finally, in the cosmological mirror even the earth itself dwindles to an invisible speck in the chilly vastnesses of intergalactic space.

How, we may ask ourselves, can this be the way of truth, when it renders invisible the things we know most surely and value most dearly about ourselves as human beings? Is it any wonder if some of the more sensitive among us recoil with horror from the whole enterprise of human science, as both a pretentious fraud and a menace to human dignity? Their suspicions may be reinforced by the suggestions of anti-religious popularisers of science that the Christian view of man in particular has been 'outdated' by the truths revealed in the scientific mirror.

From the biologist Desmond Morris, for example, they get a picture of man as 'essentially a naked ape'. By the behavioural psychologist B. F. Skinner they are assured that accounts of human nature in religious categories are merely 'pre-scientific' attempts to explain what behavioural psychology will soon (if not just yet) understand fully in its own terms. And by the molecular biologist Jacques Monod they are expressly urged to abandon religious belief on the ground that man and all his works are the meaningless product of 'pure chance', and any other view a relic of 'animistic superstition'.

Is it merely wounded vanity that makes Christians and others object to such remarks? Does our age-old sense of the dignity of man depend on keeping ourselves ignorant of what science can reveal about our nature and origins? Would we perhaps be better off without the power – and the responsibility – that comes with increased scientific understanding of what makes us tick? Does not a mechanistic scientific approach inevitably lead to meaninglessness in the end? Above all, is not the Christian assessment of our worth and significance fundamentally at odds with the objective analyses of man attempted by the human sciences? These are the main questions that will occupy us in the following chapters. They are not simple; and they touch raw nerves of concern that demand sensitive treatment. I may as well confess now that my answer to each and all of them will be 'No'. It is true enough that the methods we use in the human sciences have their necessary blind spots, and that they systematically miss some of the most important points about our human nature. As we shall see, some of them may even offer special temptations to their practitioners to take a manipulative and disloyal attitude to the community that supports them. But I see no basis for the idea that the *truths* they reveal offer any essential threat to the dignity of man. Indeed, I shall argue that the mechanistic understanding they bring is rather something to be humbly welcomed and responsibly applied, not least by

Christians; and that it tends neither to meaninglessness nor to any lessening of the awesome significance given to our personal lives in the teaching of the Bible.

Why Human Science?

Several different motives in fact lie behind the huge efforts being made today to understand man himself in scientific terms. First, of course, there is the challenge to our basic intellectual curiosity offered by the most complex organized system known to us. How does it work? Where has it come from? How does it relate to other systems we know about? Linked with this is the hope, at least in some quarters, that in the process of understanding our own machinery we may pick up some useful hints for the design of artificial mechanisms to do similar jobs for us. A second motive often expressed is the desire to 'understand ourselves'. We are each in charge of a powerful biological-psychological mechanism that we hardly know how to control. It can easily get out of hand, doing damage to itself and to others. Like a driver backing a lorry down a narrow entry, we feel we should value any feedback we can get from an outsider's standpoint. As we shall see in later chapters, there can be situations where such feedback is at best misleading and at worst destructive or manipulative; but in principle the incentive is clear enough.

The most general motive, however, which takes us back to Bacon's original appeal, is that of simple compassion for our fellow men. The world is full of unhappy people who suffer from manifest or subtle defects, hereditary or otherwise, in their physical or mental capacities. Can scientific understanding lead perhaps to prevention or cure of these conditions? We are only beginning to realize how social and other factors in early life can influence for good or ill the development of the human personality. Can we do better for our children by taking these more consciously into account? Many of our fellow citizens have acute problems of addiction, or of habitual wrongdoing which in their better moments they would fain give up. Can any help be found for them in a deeper understanding of the mechanics of habit-forming and habit-breaking? All of us are exposed constantly to a complex interplay of the influences we exert on one another, whose effects we only dimly understand. If we knew more about the exquisitely delicate structures in which our personalities are embodied,[1] might we not hope to deal more tenderly and to communicate more effectively with one another in everyday family and community life?

If at this point some readers feel that we are treading uncomfortably close to the province reserved in Christian theology for the grace of God, I would beg them to be patient. For the moment I only want to argue that there are many humane reasons for wishing the human sciences a rapid and successful development: reasons which go far beyond idle curiosity, and owe nothing to an unworthy desire to manipulate and control our fellow men, or to destroy their dignity. In view of this it may at first seem surprising that the rise of the human sciences has evoked so much suspicion and hostility among 'humanists', including even those with no belief in God. It would be superficial, I think, to put this down simply to the recent decline in the popularity of science in the wake of atomic warfare, or to the natural envy of the non-scientist towards any discipline in which reliable knowledge can (with admitted ups and downs) be cumulatively established. The basic problem goes deeper. When a mapmaker turns his instruments on his own camp and its inhabitants, his activities can have awkward consequences which have no parallel while he is mapping the world outside. In place of the neutrality of the detached spectator, he now enjoys – or suffers – the more ambivalent relationship of observer-participant. This can sometimes prove uncomfortable both for him and his fellow-campers, for reasons which will become clear if we first go back for a moment to the roots of the scientific approach.

Learning to be Puzzled

Science is often thought of as a systematic way of finding answers to questions about the world around us; and so it is. What is less often realized is that the modern scientific enterprise really began with the discovery of *new kinds of questions* to ask. In the Aristotelian tradition as it came down to the Middle Ages, most of the questions we call scientific would have been dismissed as pointless. Why does fire rise, and a stone fall? – Obviously, a good Aristotelian would say, because each has its natural resting place: fire in the heavens, a stone at the centre of the earth; so the flight of a stone to the ground is as 'natural' as that of a bird to its nest. Why must the motions of the heavenly bodies be circular? – Because the heavens are the realm of unchanging perfection, and only circular motion is perfect and unchanging. Why does an acorn sprout and grow? – In order to become an oak. So ran educated 'common sense' at the time; and in such a climate our kind of science could never get off the ground.

We must remind ourselves that the people who reasoned in this rationalistic way were not a whit our inferiors in intellect – indeed some of them were probably brighter than most scientists around today. What hindered them in developing experimental science as we know it was not lack of brains, but basically that they were *not puzzled* by the things that came to puzzle Newton and Boyle and those who followed them: they had not learned to *recognize the oddity* of the processes they took for granted.

As the Dutch historian of Science, R. Hooykaas, has recently emphasized,[2] there were important religious as well as secular factors at work in the awakening of curiosity that gave rise to science as we know it. Men who read the Bible for themselves discovered in it a conception of nature so different from the semi-divine 'Nature' of the Greek philosophers that their imagination began to feel free to play in areas that previous generations had thought to be forbidden. As we already noted, curiosity to 'read the Book of nature' was for

Francis Bacon not only legitimate (because nature was a mere creature, like man himself) but also praiseworthy, as an act of worship and obedience to the One who had written that Book and had commanded men to subdue (in humility) the created order. Thus despite the notorious skirmishes between such stalwarts as Galileo or Giordano Bruno and the Aristotelian religious establishment, consistently biblical religion remained not merely in harmony with the new scientific attitude but a powerful reinforcer of it, the great chemist Robert Boyle being himself perhaps the best exemplar.[3]

But this is a digression. For our present purpose the point is that the development of any new science requires a deliberate effort (or at least a readiness) to *see the familiar in an unfamiliar way*, so that our curiosity may be stirred by the oddity of things we have hitherto taken for granted. Perhaps the comparative lateness of the development of the human sciences reflects the greater difficulty we have as human beings in 'standing back from ourselves' so as to be struck by what needs explaining in what we take for granted about ourselves. As we shall now see, this effort after detachment has a special kind of cost in the human sciences which has no parallel in others, and which may in large measure account for, if not justify, the hostility that these sciences have attracted.

The Costs of Detachment

At the start of a Church of Scotland service in my home town many years ago, a small boy's voice piped shrilly from behind a horrified parent's hand: 'Why is he standing up there with a black nightie on, Margaret MacDonald's father?' It was his first exposure to public worship in the Presbyterian manner; and he had still the eyes to see something odd in the behaviour and garb of Margaret MacDonald's otherwise perfectly normal parent. For the rest of the congregation, it would have needed more explanation if the worthy minister had appeared without his customary robe, and still more if he had failed to mount the pulpit. For them he was merely fulfilling expectations. There was nothing to be puzzled about in that.

Each of us, as normally brought up human beings, has a whole rich repertoire of expected behaviour that we exercise almost without thinking. For example, as I leave home on a typical morning you might see me wave good-bye to my wife, smile to the youngest member of the family as I drive past the school crossing, and call at the shop to pay a bill. You would normally have no difficulty in understanding each of these actions of mine in terms of what I, as a conscious human being, am trying or intending to do. Certainly it would never occur to you to find them puzzling. What more, you might ask, is needed by way of explanation? It is all quite obvious to common sense.

The trained response of the human scientist, however, is to ask himself: supposing I knew nothing about the human customs of waving upper extremities or pulling facial muscles as signals to other human beings, or of driving a car, or of incurring and honouring obligations, what *then* might strike me as puzzling about these performances? How far could I account for them by analogy with other phenomena with which I am familiar, whether in physics, or physiology, or automation engineering, or the behaviour of animals, or whatever? Could I produce a guidebook for the interested spectator from another planet which would help him to integrate the phenomena of human behaviour with his scientific understanding of other natural events on earth, even if he knew nothing at first hand about what it feels like to be a man?

You will see at once that there are some deep-going snags in this approach. First, and most obviously, no human student of science can put himself in the place of a fully detached spectator. We all know at first hand more than we can put into words about what it means to be human. If we see a man getting angry, for example, we can *feel* what it must be like, and we depend a good deal on this kind of 'tacit' knowledge (as Polanyi calls it) to make sense of what we are watching. So at the root of our scientific question there is an element of pretence, almost of hypocrisy. Even when we do our best to play the spectator game strictly by the rules, we start with an unfair and un-spectatorlike advantage; and we end as fully-involved human beings with the same gamut of needs and desires and responsibilities and potentialities as those we study. The human scientist is always at risk of seeming to want to have his cake and yet – willy nilly – to eat it too.

Secondly (and for a related reason), even to raise some of the questions that would be appropriate for a pure spectator-scientist can in certain circumstances bring in something very like *bad faith*. To start with a simple example, suppose that for the first time in our lives we are watching two people at a game of chess. 'I wish I still had my Queen on that square,' says player A. 'Why don't you lift it up and put it there?' asks the innocent spectator. 'Don't be silly, I can't do that – it would be cheating,' says A – echoed emphatically by B, who joins A in looking askance at anyone who would even raise such a question. We feel embarrassed and a little unfairly judged. Our question, if we had kept it to ourselves, would have been a perfectly legitimate one about the social psychology of chess-playing, admitting of a straightforward answer in terms of what it means for two people to abide by the rules of chess. But while A is playing his role, even to contemplate the possibility of making an illegal move would for him be inconsistent with his commitment. It is not surprising, then, that for him our scientific spectator's question sounds like an invitation to consider cheating, to be rejected as basically immoral.

An even stronger reason for rejecting the perspective of the detached spectator applies in a card game such as Bridge where, unless each player is prevented from seeing the cards of the others, the game cannot be played as intended. It would be absurd to claim that because as spectators we 'know the truth', therefore the players morally ought to wish to know that truth too. They would rightly scorn us as merely inviting one or more of them to break the rules that define the game. However true it may be that 'the onlooker sees more of the game', in this case the knowledge of the onlooker is not the kind of knowledge that the players *could* have at the time and still play the game according to the rules. Thus, oddly enough, what the spectator-scientist knows in this case *is not knowledge-for-players-as-such*, since if they knew it, they would cease to be players in the defined sense. In this case, then, it is both morally right and rational for the players to shield themselves from the spectator scientist's knowledge of their situation. They have a *right not to know* what he knows, even though it be the truth. To thrust it on them would be the action of a mere spoil-sport.

In these examples, of course, the obligations of the players last only until the game is over, when everyone can in retrospect share the spectator-view of their activities. A more serious snag crops up if the human scientist wants to study in detachment the activities of the community to which he himself belongs. In this case the 'game' is normally for life. Certain mutual expectations are inseparable from membership of a normal human community – for example, that debts will be honoured and promises kept. Yet the human scientist, when practising his profession, must adopt a detached attitude to these expectations, studying all forms of human behaviour as if he found them potentially odd and in need of explanation, even though he is also (or is expected to be) himself one of the players-for-life in the social game. Confronted with the spectacle of an honourable man who suffers loss in order to keep a promise, he may understand perfectly well the personal reason for the action: an honourable man would do nothing else. Yet for scientific purposes the human scientist must act as if this were no sufficient explanation, and ask himself (for example) what social reinforcements, or what neural processes in the man's brain, were operative to bring about this end-result. In order to do this, he may have at least in imagination to withdraw himself from the social game, taking a standpoint that allows his imagination to contemplate, among other things, the possibility of ignoring the rules.

Here, obviously, there lies danger. In the first place, if such speculations are overheard, especially by the man whom the scientist is studying, they are liable to create an impression of amorality (if not immorality) that can hardly be expected to deepen the trust and confidence with which he is regarded by his fellows. Secondly, when the human scientist finds himself in a similar situation of obligation, he may in fact suffer stronger temptations than others would to bend or ignore the rules of the game. Because he has habitually to break, or at least suspend, *our* rules in order to play *his* spectator-game, he has to take special precautions to ensure that the habit of switching to his professional spectator-standpoint does not overcome his scruples as a fellow human being.

Lest this seem over-dramatized, let me cite the real-life case of a widely respected anthropologist, a specialist in Red Indian culture, who at a scientific conference some years ago told us all frankly of a 'dilemma' in which he found himself. Having gained some exciting information about certain tribal customs at the cost of swearing himself to lifelong secrecy, he had begun to wonder whether he might not have a 'duty to science' (to publish his findings) which would of course conflict with the oath he had sworn to the tribespeople! He assured us that such 'dilemmas' are quite common in social science; and it is not difficult to believe him.

Finally, to the extent that his spectator-knowledge gives him the power (at least in principle) to shape the behaviour or the beliefs of his fellows without their knowledge, the human scientist may be specially tempted to assume the attitude, if not the role, of a manipulator rather than a servant of the community. The image of the omnipotent 'predictor behind the scenes' beloved of science fiction writers has very little basis in scientific reality; but for the sociologist in particular the dilemma is in principle inescapable. As Dr. J. A. Walter puts it in a recent article:[4] 'The sociologist cannot be a scientist if this means he has to cease being a participant and to extract himself from society so that he may observe without bias. On the other hand the sociologist wants to say something more than the novelist and the artist, for he does not want merely to add to the pile of personal views about society. This problem has not been solved by sociologists.' As we shall see in Chapter 3, the social scientist cannot entirely escape from his manipulative role even by deciding not to publish, since that decision may sometimes play a predictable part in shaping the course of his society, and will thus itself be manipulative.

In face of all this, you would perhaps expect me to argue that no imaginable benefits derivable from a science of man could be worth the moral risks, both to the human community and to the would-be scientists. Are not the Morrises, the Skinners, the Monods of our day, you might ask, a standing example of the mess that our thinking gets into when we treat man as an object of detached scrutiny, rather than a moral being with sacred rights and responsibilities in the sight of his Creator? But to argue in this way, I believe, would be to mistake the point, and would seem particularly wrongheaded from the standpoint of biblical Christianity. Let it be granted that there is some justification for the hostility and mistrust felt by many people (both Christian and non-Christian) towards the sciences of man and their practitioners. The risks we have touched on are real and non-trivial, and we shall be returning to the subject in later chapters. But despite these risks, and despite the occasional unjustified sallies by anti-religious apologists in the name of human science, I want to argue that Christian believers in particular have the best of reasons to seek a scientific understanding of human nature.

CHAPTER 2

Man in a Scientific Mirror

What then does it mean, and what does it not mean, to approach the study of man scientifically? We are concerned in this book mainly with aspects of human science affecting our ideas of human dignity, and I hope that you will forgive me if I select only a few key points for emphasis.

Levels of Explanation

First, any scientist approaching such a complex system as a human being must quite deliberately choose a level (or at least, one level at a time) at which to work. By 'choosing a level' I mean something forced upon us by the complexity of the situation, which is easily illustrated in areas which have nothing to do with human science. If you wanted to study an aeroplane scientifically, for instance, you might choose the level of aerodynamics and consider how it manages to stay up in the air; you might take the standpoint of the metallurgist and ask how its materials cope with stresses; or you might adopt an information-engineering approach and analyze the control system by which the pilot (or the automatic pilot) keeps it on an even keel. At each of these levels, quite different scientific questions can be asked and answered, each in its own terms.

Or take another example, perhaps nearer to the mark for our purpose. Suppose you came across a computer, knowing nothing about it, and wanted to understand it scientifically. You might decide to start by studying the conduction of current in the copper that links its components together; alternatively, you could tackle the electronics of the transistors and other computing elements that process information in it; or again, you might study it as a functioning whole, trying to learn what is meant by programming, and how to recognize when a problem has been solved.

For the same reason, and in the same general sense, *man* as a phenomenon requires many levels of analysis to do him justice. The science of man inevitably provides us with a whole spectrum of different accounts, each framed in categories appropriate to its own level.[5] The key question is how these various possible scientific accounts are related to one another, and to our personal experience as human beings.

To someone brought up as I was in physics, you might think it would come naturally to insist that the 'ultimate' or 'fundamental' explanation of a human action, as of anything else, must be found in the physical forces between the molecules concerned. If a physiologist were to account for the action in terms of nerve impulses, or a psychologist in terms of conditioning, or a theologian in terms of sinful inclinations, what they say could in that case be accepted only as at best a shorthand for the full physical story, if not rejected altogether as superfluous verbiage. According to this view, only where physical explanation was impossible could any other account be taken seriously in its own right. Otherwise, the whole thing could be explained away as 'nothing but' the mindless motion of molecules.

The fallacy underlying this presupposition (to which I once gave the rude name of 'nothing-buttery') is now generally recognized. Take the example of a machine such as a wrist watch. Nothing could be more clearly a candidate for complete explanation in physical terms; yet as Michael Polanyi[6] has pointed out, a purely physical explanation in terms of molecules would *have no concepts* for the *functions* of the various parts. However complete in its own terms, it would systematically miss the points that a functional explanation would make.

Or take again the example of a computer solving a mathematical problem. In theory its behaviour might be completely explained either in terms of its molecules and their physical motions, or in terms of its transistors and their electronic operations; but neither of these accounts could make the same points or convey the same understanding as a mathematician's explanation of the computer's activity.

Clearly then it is possible in some cases for an explanation to be complete in its own terms without either excluding or making superfluous another explanation at a different level. A watch, or a computing machine, are examples of common situations which require explanations at *more than one level*, in quite different categories, to do them justice.

For exactly the same reasons, I shall argue, we need a whole hierarchy of levels and categories of explanation if we are to do justice to the richness of the nature of man. There is no justification whatever for insisting that explanations at lower levels must be incomplete in their own terms if a higher-level explanation is true: that higher levels are valid only as long as there are 'gaps' in explanations at lower levels.

Note that to call a level 'higher' does not imply that explanations at that level are always to be preferred. The point is only that if a story at a 'higher' level is true, some corresponding story must be true at the 'lower' level – but the converse is not the case. For example, if it is true that a computer is solving a mathematical problem (higher level), it must also be true that corresponding currents are flowing through some of its wires (lower level); but not all flows of current through the wires of a computer signify the solving of a problem. Similarly, in brain science we assume as a working hypothesis that whenever a human being has a conscious experience (higher level), some corresponding physical activity takes place in his brain (lower level); but not all brain activity is associated with conscious experience.

As we noted in Chapter 1, it is only to be expected that while we are engaged in this 'analysis by levels' we lose sight of man himself. A familiar analogy would be the work involved in restoring an old portrait. The expert takes his microscope or his high-powered lens, and some very fine implements, and focuses on a particular chip of pigment which he tries to build up to the shape he thinks it had before. While he is doing this, he is obviously unable to see the portrait as such. This is so commonplace that one would think it hardly needs saying, were it not quite commonly ignored or misrepresented both in lay reactions to human science and in the propaganda put out by some of the popularists on the scientific side. The impression often given is that what you see while you are using your scientific instruments is 'the real thing'; and that there is something illusory, or at least something not quite decent or solid, about what you thought you saw before you brought them in. The truth is that it is the disappearance of man himself from the scientific picture that is illusory. So far from being alarming, it is the most natural thing in the world. It is equally natural that what you do see will vary with your standpoint and your 'viewing distance', just as happens with a painting. The point to remember is that when this happens it is you who are changing, not the reality in front of you: the reality remains just the same. So when the scientist adopts a level of analysis that has no room for the human, moral or spiritual aspects or attributes of man, none of this affects the reality of the man in front of him. The man continues as a conscious moral human being just as he always was – unless, of course, the scientist in his probing and measuring were actually to interfere with his role-playing capacities. (By 'playing a role' here I do not mean anything like 'play-acting', but simply exercising our capacities for sensitive and responsible relationships: the gracious recognition of obligations and mutual expectations.)

Note that with such a hierarchy of levels there is no question of keeping the different explanations in 'watertight compartments': what someone has called 'conceptual apartheid'. Although their categories are different and they are not making the same statements, by calling them hierarchic we commit ourselves to the view that there is a definite *correspondence* between them. In particular, no change can take place in the conscious experience reported in a higher-level story without some corresponding change in the stories to be told at the lower levels (though again, not conversely). On this view, the way to an integrated understanding of man is not to hunt for gaps in the scientific picture into which entities like 'the soul' might fit, but rather to discover, if we can, how the stories at different levels correlate.

To show how this works out in practice, let me give you an example from my own field of brain research. At Keele we are interested particularly in the processes of seeing and hearing. At the physical level, we study these by recording electrical signals produced in the brain when patterns of light or sound are received. But the human brain is unique in offering us another source of clues to the processes going on in its depths, in the conscious experience of the man whose brain it is. To take advantage of this we also use the methods of experimental psychology to study what people see or hear when presented with special test signals. Optical illusions, for example, turn out to be particularly informative in this connection, revealing a number of clues, which we might never have discovered otherwise, to the way in which the brain reacts to messages from the eyes.

How then do we tie together the information from these very different levels? Not by finding any simple *translations* from one to the other, but rather by looking to see what sort of *change* at the physical level corresponds to a *change* in conscious experience or vice versa. It would make no sense to look for a description in physical terms which would *say the same thing* as a description in terms of what is experienced; but the two descriptions must say *corresponding* things if both are correct. They are neither *identical* nor *independent*, but rather *complementary*.[5]

Although the technicalities need not concern us, it is worth mentioning that in the human brain we have to deal with a system of nerve cells and connections numbering tens of thousands of millions, so that any idea of keeping track of all of its activity at once (let alone predicting its future) is completely ruled out. Nobody could live long enough even to make the necessary observations! Our own brain capacity, the capacity of the computers that we could build, and for that matter the interference we would cause to the brain by our attempts to record from its cells, all set irreducible limits to the prospects of analyzing brain activity in detail. Any scientific understanding we can hope to achieve must be restricted to minute samples of the population, or else be expressed in terms of relatively crude descriptions based on averages over large numbers of cells. By the same token, the best correlations we can hope to achieve between anyone's physical brain activity and his conscious experience must inevitably be rather approximate, leaving more of the details unknown than known.

When we come to general principles, the picture is less gloomy, though our ignorance is still vast. It may not be long, for example, before the physical changes that store information in the brain (and so underlie our power to learn and remember) have been identified. Already we have evidence suggesting that the 'code symbols' of memory may be located at the minute junction points or 'gateways' at which nerve fibres make contact so that cells can influence each other. There are hundreds or even thousands of such junction points strung along the branching fibres of a typical nerve cell, often visible under a high-powered microscope as tiny swellings or spines. If these gateways change their physical properties according to the signals passing through them, becoming more 'open' or 'shut', the millions of millions of changes made in this way could be more than sufficient to record all the information that a man has to remember in a lifetime.

Conversely, we are beginning to learn how people's sensations and moods can be affected by changes imposed on the brain from outside, either by means of drugs in the blood supply, or by electric currents passed along thin wires stuck into the brain through the skull. The effects are usually very crude, because the drugs or current will tend to affect thousands of nerve cells indiscriminately; and the popular idea of some tyrant effecting precise remote control of people's thoughts and feelings in this way is sheer science fiction (see Chapter 4). Nevertheless, even the results to date have provided some important clues to the functioning of the brain; and they are of interest here because they illustrate further the intimate two-way relationship that exists between the physical activity of the brain and the conscious experience of the individual. It means not only that mental activity is represented by detectable physical changes in the brain, but also that minute physical changes introduced in the brain's pattern of activity can give rise to changes in conscious experience.

Integration

How then can the scientist hope to tie together the information from two or more levels? What does this mean? We have been looking at the view we get when we approach the brain with the eye of an engineer, studying it as a system for communicating information, associating information, and controlling action. Let me emphasize again that at present our knowledge is very fragmentary, and the processes we understand are only tiny spots of light in the great darkness that shrouds the detailed functioning of the brain. But just supposing that we were able to achieve an understanding of its workings similar to that which a computer engineer has of the works of a computer, how could we set about integrating that understanding with, say, a religious view of human nature? I have already hinted that it would be fruitless and misguided to pin our hopes on the discovery of phenomena in the brain that disobey physical laws. Because there will always be enormous gaps in our knowledge, nobody who postulates such phenomena could be refuted; but I do not think they would provide the kind of integration we need. Instead, I suggest that we could best hope to integrate the engineering level with the personal level by painstakingly discovering what causal relationships at the two levels *correspond*, as far as we can tell. So, for example, we would not try to do what the French philosopher Descartes suggested, looking in the brain for signs of non-physical forces exerted by the soul; but it would make sense to look in the brain (if we could) for physical happenings whose pattern was correlated with that of conscious activities such as examining-one's-motives, or making-up-one's-mind. Examining-one's-motives is a conscious activity with mental consequences, for all of which it would make sense to seek *correlates* in the organizing system of the brain. (Notice, however, that in order to find a correlate we may have to be prepared to leave hyphens between such expressions as 'examining-one's-motives'. Examining motives, as an activity, may have a direct mechanistic correlate; whereas 'motives' as entities may have none.)

This leads me to one further point. There has been a long tradition in Christian thinking which suggests that man must be thought of as made of either two 'parts' or three 'parts' if we are to do justice to what the Bible has to say about him. Man is thought of as body plus mind plus spirit, or perhaps body plus mind, or body plus soul. I venture to suggest that if you look again at the biblical data you will find it equally consistent, and in some ways easier to do justice to those data, to emphasize rather the *unity* of man, thinking of body, mind and spirit as distinct *aspects* of that unity. I recognize of course that there are metaphors in the New Testament that might be taken to support the first view. For example, we are 'clothed' with our bodies, our body is a 'tent', and so forth. But arguments from metaphors must always be subject to the test of data: God's data. It is God who will hold us responsible for doing justice to those data; and I confess that to me the two-way relationship between brain activity and conscious experience seems really too close to justify taking metaphors in terms of 'clothing' or 'tents' as proving that the soul is an invisible 'substance' *inhabiting* the body. The data rather suggest that man is at one and the same time (i) a body, (ii) a 'living soul' or conscious being (the Hebrew word is *nephesh*, also used of lower animals) and (iii) a spiritual being, in the sense that he can be called to account by God, can come to know God, and can enjoy the gift of eternal life with God. If we want to integrate our scientific understanding of man at various levels with the biblical view, I believe we will find ourselves less hampered, and closer both to the biblical and to the scientific data, if we think of man as a unity with a number of complementary aspects rather than as a kind of bodily vehicle with a 'mind' sitting in some cerebral driving seat.

CHAPTER 3

How Not to Defend Human Dignity

I have been arguing that the scientific way of trying to acquire solid knowledge, by experiment and hypothesis from a detached standpoint, is not merely compatible with the biblical view of the natural world, both historically and logically, but positively encouraged by it. I have also argued that if we try to use the scientific mirror to look at man himself we must expect quite naturally to lose sight, for the time being, of man as man. The idea that a complete explanation at a given scientific level necessarily debunks all others, or makes them superfluous, we saw to be a fallacy. My suggestion has been that if we think of man as a unity, with a conscious personal 'inner' aspect and various 'outer' aspects which can be studied by scientists from a detached standpoint, then we will find ourselves able to do full justice to the biblical claims about human nature; and that we need to recognize all these different aspects, scientific and otherwise, if we are to do justice to all that it means to be a man.

A couple of centuries ago it might have been tempting to a certain type of theologian to go further, and try to make arguments for the existence of God out of the latest findings of the human sciences. Since then, however, the cogency of such arguments from science in matters of religious belief has been strongly questioned, and they are now largely out of favour among Christians. Ironically enough, in our time it seems to be the anti-religious apologists who are keeping up the tradition of seeking illicit support in scientific data for their metaphysical beliefs (or unbeliefs). If it was clearly wishful thinking on the part of our forefathers to imagine that they could disprove atheism by scientific discoveries, it is the more remarkable to observe the 'wishful *un*thinking' of those who nowadays seek to discredit Christianity by similarly bogus appeals to science.

In this chapter we will be taking a critical look at some representative samples of anti-religious propaganda claiming the prestige of science, all of it aimed directly or indirectly at the dignity of man. But my purpose will not be just to uncover the logical fallacies in such attacks. What concerns me even more is the risk that Christians and others may be confused by the nothing-buttery of their opponents into directing their fire at quite the wrong targets, seeking to defend human dignity by counter-arguments which may be at best irrelevant and at worst actually harmful, because they unwittingly accept and reinforce the mistaken presuppositions that are causing the trouble. Until these mistakes are recognized, much that is true and valuable in the scientific picture of man risks being neglected to our loss.

The Scientific Bogey

The kind of writing that creates or supports this threatening image of human science is usually deliberately intemperate in tone. On the jacket of Desmond Morris's book *The Naked Ape*[7] for example – a book which made quite a stir about 10 years ago – we are told that 'since he first became intellectually aware, man has indulged in lofty and exhaustive enquiries into his own nature. Now this ethological analysis by an eminent zoologist *puts him firmly in his place* (my italics) alongside the 192 other species of apes and monkeys, among which man is most easily distinguished by the nakedness of his skin.' Or take the foreword by R. L. Travers to Richard Dawkins's recent book[8] *The Selfish Gene*. 'Most human thinkers', he says, 'regard the chimp as a malformed irrelevant oddity, while seeing themselves as stepping stones to the Almighty. To an evolutionist this cannot be so. There exists no objective basis on which to elevate one species above another.' The jacket of the same book declares that 'Richard Dawkins introduces us to ourselves as we *really* are, throwaway survival machines for our immortal genes. Man is a gene machine, blindly programmed to preserve its selfish genes.' (my italics)

Given the provocative tone of statements like these, it is perhaps not surprising if to some people the science of human behaviour appears as a bogey that threatens religious values in general, and human dignity in particular. The fault however is not all on one side. It is questionable whether so many unbelievers today would regard science as a support for their atheism if there had been no suggestion from some Christians to the same effect. By the same token, I fear that some of the hostility to human science on the part of defenders of human dignity arises from a tendency to base that dignity on various sorts of wrong foundation.

Let me start with some negatives. First, I suggest that true dignity is not something a man has by virtue of his shape, or size, or the stuff he is made of, or his mechanical complexity, or his ancestry. It is rather something which depends on and reflects his *capacity for inter-personal roles or relationships*: specifically, his capacity for accepting and fulfilling obligations and mutual expectations, both to his fellow men and (the Christian would say) to his Creator. Secondly, I suggest that dignity is not really a meaningful attribute of *man* as a species, but rather an attribute of *men*, individually or collectively, as *agents*: as people who live, think and act either with or without dignity. Thirdly, I would argue that dignity has to do with the way a man *uses* his social repertoire – his powers of communication with his fellows and with God, his intelligence, his capacity for love or hate, for worship, for moral choice and so on – rather than simply with its extent or its elaborateness. It is not the number of different things he can do or the strength of his capacities that matters, so much as the appropriateness, effectiveness and sensitivity with which he uses the repertoire he has. Fourthly, if you follow me in this last suggestion, you may agree that dignity in this sense is not unique to the human species: it can perfectly well be an attribute of lower animals as well. A good-going chimp is worthy of the respect due to one who uses competently his chimply repertoire. Would that all human beings qualified for respect by the same criterion!

Finally, and positively, for the biblical theist our human dignity arises essentially from *what our Creator has told us* that he expects of us – the role that he has created us to fulfil. Here, for example, is John Smith – an honest yeoman living, let us say, in the days before technology and over-population had distorted the priorities of the country dweller. He leads a modest but dignified self-supporting existence as a member of an appreciative community, responding worthily to the various claims made on him, and enjoying the trust and confidence of his fellows. He has his dignity. He is respected and knows it; and he respects others.

On what then does John's dignity stand? Could it be reduced by discovering any particular facts about the material of his body, such as the extent to which it conforms to physical laws, or the resemblances between its components and those of any other body, human or animal? John Smith and his fellows would laugh off all such considerations – and rightly – as quite beside the point. Is it then a question of pedigree? He may in fact be the son of a respected father; but surely his dignity could be no less if he had earned his respected place in the community without that advantage? Is it a matter of intelligence? Would his dignity necessarily be greater if he had an IQ 50 points higher? Or, if you discovered that his IQ was lower than that of some of his fellows, would his dignity now be any less? Surely not. The world is full of clever people without dignity, and of humble but dignified folk who have no pretensions to brilliance.

No. The plain fact, to which all the world's great literature bears witness, is that it is the manner in which John Smith exercises his capacities, great or small, that determines the dignity to be attributed to him. Only what interferes with, or limits, a man's capacity to play his particular human role to the full can damage his dignity. As we shall see in later chapters, science can in some forms be misused to do just this; but although various scientific ways of analyzing a man may necessarily take him out of commission for the time being as a role player, the analysis *as such* does nothing to damage his dignity. If human dignity inheres in the roles that a man can play, then to adopt a mode of analysis that renders the role invisible only allows you to lose sight of his dignity, not to debunk it.

False Moves

You can probably recognize now the false moves in the battle for human dignity, against which I believe we must be on our guard. The first is the move in the direction of anti-science, hostility to science as such, to which I have already referred. The growth of undisciplined credulity, the lowering of standards of evidence, the encouragement of fads for pseudo-science and irrational self-expression and so on, all in the name of what is called 'sensitivity' – these trends are something to be resisted by all (whether scientists or not) who have the preservation of true human dignity at heart. For if we wilfully abandon our critical faculties, if we wilfully lower the standards we set for accepting claims presented to us as true, then in whatever name we do it we are destroying rather than enhancing our dignity. Let me add that it is surely possible to be artistically sensitive – as sensitive as any human being could wish to be – without being irrational! It may be that irrationality is statistically linked with artistic or other sensitivity (I do not know); but it is certainly not a sufficient condition for sensitivity, and I do not think it is even a necessary one.

The second false move against which we must warn ourselves is what I am going to call 'reverse nothing-buttery'. By this I mean agreeing with the opponents of human dignity that a complete scientific explanation at some level would indeed banish the mind, or human responsibility, or God, or whatever it might be from the scene, but then basing our hopes on the fact that scientific explanations are in their nature always incomplete. The scientist can only *sample*, say these would-be defenders of man. There are always gaps in a scientific explanation, and therefore we can relax, because the enemy of human dignity can never fully prove his case.

As I argued in the last chapter, this strategy is both dangerous and misguided. It is dangerous, because as has often been pointed out in other contexts, if you argue in reliance on the present gaps in a scientific picture, your argument can last only as long as your cherished gaps are unfilled. And it is misguided, because although I believe it is technically inevitable that there must be gaps in any scientific picture, nevertheless to suggest that it is the *gaps* which betoken or give important evidence for the dignity of man would be to obscure the true basis for that dignity.

In this chapter I want to highlight these dangers by considering two or three typical issues in more detail. You will recognize them at once if I label them *Man and beast*, *Behaviourism* and *Determinism*. In each case we shall take a cool look at the way in which scientific theories or facts have been made to sound like a threat to the moral and spiritual understanding of human nature, and see which are the false moves to avoid in countering such attacks.

Man and Beast

We may start by taking a second look at the inflammatory claims we considered earlier. 'Since he first became intellectually aware, man has indulged in lofty and exhaustive enquiries into his own nature.' If we ignore the unscientific sneer in the word 'lofty', that is innocuously true. 'Now this ethological analysis by an eminent zoologist puts him firmly in his place alongside the 192 other species of apes and monkeys, among which man is most easily distinguished by the nakedness of his skin.' Cut out the unscientific 'firmly', and this also collapses to an innocent statement of fact. If you turn the scientific mirror on man at the level of zoological analysis, trying to classify his bodily type, you will bracket him with the apes and monkeys. Certainly if you have a row of pelts in front of you, and one of them is naked, that tells you which is the human one. What then is all the fuss about? The overall impression given, that some important blow is dealt by zoology to human dignity, is simply bogus: an illusion artfully created by the way the facts are put. The truth is not that zoology reveals facts that discredit John Smith's dignity, but only that while we are using the scientific mirror for zoological purposes we have temporarily to ignore the facts that reveal his dignity.

Then there was that remark by Travers: 'Most human thinkers regard the chimp as a malformed irrelevant oddity, while seeing themselves as stepping stones to the Almighty.' The first part may or may not be true of 'most human thinkers'; but when the second part is purged of its unscientific venom, it presumably refers to the fact that many human thinkers, especially in the biblical tradition, have seen their fellow men, not as 'stepping stones to the Almighty', but as creatures specially equipped and personally called by the Creator to come to know and love and serve him and be cleaned up by him for a relationship with eternal consequences. Now notice what follows. 'To an evolutionist *this cannot be so. There exists no objective basis* on which to elevate one species above another' – (my italics). Why cannot it be so? Travers can only mean that the level of evolutionary biology offers no criteria for making such an assessment. This is true enough; but to conclude from that that no basis exists at *any* level is simply a mistake in logic; and to pretend that any scientific data *rule out* the biblical assessment is blatantly false.

What then of the claim that genetic analysis 'introduces us to ourselves as we *really* are'? It has often been pointed out that when a man says 'really', he is bringing in metaphysics by the back door. Viewed in the mirror of the geneticist, no doubt all we are (at that level) can be described as 'throwaway survival machines for our immortal genes'. From the imaginary standpoint of the gene, the function of the human body is just to make sure that the genes that have programmed its development are passed on; it fails in that function if they are not. But to suggest that the view at this level has some special claim to 'reality', in *opposition* to the views at other levels, is quite baseless. (Dawkins himself, it should be said, seems more perceptive than his blurb writer, and repeatedly denies any reductionist intentions in using this metaphor.)

I hope it is now clear how inept it would be for defenders of human dignity to respond to passages such as these by attacking human science as such. Scientists can of course get their facts wrong. It is easy to terrify the layman by bending the scientific mirror so that the image of man presented is distorted and false; and even the most carefully constructed scientific picture is likely in due course to become obsolete. But what is objectionable in the statements we have been looking at has nothing to do with the accuracy or otherwise of their science. It is rather the impression given that their destructive metaphysical innuendos have scientific support. Purged of their illegitimately imported anti-religious overtones, there is no reason to quarrel with such statements, unless on grounds of straight scientific fact. However tentative may be our theories of the process by which John Smith's body was genetically specified, or the ancestry you would find for him if you could trace enough generations back, there is just no point at which John Smith's actual dignity would depend on denying such theories. If the evolutionary story of human origins scientifically accepted today is wrong, doubtless some other kind of story at the same scientific level waits to be discovered, and Christians have no biblical reason to pretend that they know the right one in advance. It would be particularly foolish to try to defend human dignity by denying or undervaluing the similarities that scientists are finding at various levels of analysis between man and other species.

I can imagine some defenders of human dignity objecting

to this last point. 'Are you not offering a dangerous opening to the thin end of a wedge?' they might ask. 'If practically all human capacities had some kind of dim representation in lower animals, would not the difference between man and lower animals be only a matter of degree?' To this my answer would be 'yes and no'. The point is that 'a matter of degree' can also be a matter of qualitative import. To see what I mean, imagine that a youngster finds a box containing, let us say, three or four letters of the alphabet. What can he do with them? As far as English composition is concerned, the child cannot get off the ground. But if you give the same youngster a box of 10,000 letters of the alphabet suitably assorted, he can then set up whole sentences which can be true or false, he can compose a poem, he has gained a repertoire which is qualitatively different from anything possible with just two or three. What I am suggesting is that the qualitative differences between men and beasts are not at all obliterated by acknowledging that individual capacities once thought to be unique to *homo sapiens* have their faint reflections in lower animals. If we imagine that granting this would put us on a slippery slope, so that there could be no way of stopping short of according full human dignity to all animals, I think we are making a logical mistake. This (a first cousin to 'nothing-buttery') I like to call 'thin-end-of-the-wedgery'. It is the same sort of mistake as insisting that because a child with 10,000 letters can compose a sonnet, therefore a child with two or three letters must be able to achieve something of the same sort. It is plain bad reasoning.

This said, let me repeat the earlier point that however different the capacities of beasts may be from those of men, we should not try to *underrate* their dignity. If you have ever spent some time watching a community of chimps or other higher animals at work and play, and appreciated the range of purposes that they can learn to pursue intelligently, you will know what I mean. It is just perverse to refuse to recognize a certain kind of simple animal dignity about these creatures – they fill their roles very well. In all such comparisons our duty is to be obedient to the full richness of our data as objectively as possible. It is not always easy to resist the temptation to think as tacticians of the debating field, where people are reluctant to admit even the truth for fear of giving their opponents a chance to score a point. But Christians in particular must surely see it as part of our duty to the God of truth, the God who has given beasts capacities that he knows better than we, to do objective justice to the state of knowledge as best we can.

A good example of analysis in this spirit is a book by W. H. Thorpe[9] called *Animal Nature and Human Nature* (1974). In relation to the uniqueness of man, he lists seven or eight criteria once thought to offer safe ways of distinguishing men from other animals. Animals, it was said, cannot learn, cannot plan, cannot conceptualize, have no tools and cannot use tools, have no language, cannot count, and have no artistic sense. It was also said that they have no ethical sense. Thorpe, who has spent a life-time in analyzing animal behaviour, goes patiently through the evidence that each of these statements is strictly false. He offers plenty of evidence of rudimentary ability in animals to do all of these things, including even the capacity to handle human language in a primitive form.

I remember in 1951 spending an afternoon in the company of Vicky, a famous young lady chimp who had been reared like a human baby in the Florida home of Dr. & Mrs. Hayes. The nearest that Vicky could get to pronouncing an English word was to emit a burp that sounded like 'cup' when presented with her mug. Thorpe notes that all efforts to teach chimps to *speak* have been unproductive. By using deaf and dumb sign-language, however, chimps have not only been taught to have rudimentary but purposeful child-like dialogue with a human being, but also to pass on to their offspring the game of making sign-language gestures to one another: not just mentioning words in the way that a parrot does, but using them as a means of achieving desired results. Along this line evidence has piled up that it is simply false to deny that animals can to some extent use language and do the other things on Thorpe's list. (Animals can count up to seven, it seems; and there is plenty of evidence suggesting that birds at any rate have an artistic sense.)

Thorpe, however, with characteristic balance, keeps the record straight. Even granting all these capacities, he says, 'we are left with a tremendous chasm, intellectual, artistic, technical, linguistic, moral, ethical, scientific and spiritual, between ape and man.' Moreover 'we have no clear idea as to how this gap was bridged. Man is unique in all these aspects, and we may never know how this happened.' Thorpe's book is an admirable example of the handling of scientific data in a clean scientific spirit which is neither cramped by fear on the one hand nor irresponsibly arrogant on the other.

It is perhaps worth adding that to deny the biological theory of evolution, as some of our forefathers felt it important to do, would do nothing to dispose of this issue of the similarities between man and beast. The similarities are there to be reckoned with, whatever chronological story we believe (or disbelieve) about our human ancestry. On this point again Christians should surely be in the forefront of unprejudiced efforts to establish what the data are and to follow their implications, in obedience to the Giver of them all.

Behaviourism – Positive and Negative

The term 'behaviourism' is often used in sermons and other Christian literature as if it were by definition an alternative to the spiritual view of human nature. There are doubtless people who label themselves 'behaviourists' with this intention; but if we are to think clearly it is vital to make a distinction between what might be called *positive* and *negative* behaviourism. By 'positive' behaviourism I mean simply a particular scientific method or habit of approach to the understanding of human behaviour, which looks for causal connections only between observable acts and events in the environment. By contrast, I shall use 'negative' behaviourism to mean a particular metaphysical doctrine, which is characterized by what it *denies* and is parasitic on the scientific theory and data, though in fact having no logical support from them.

Behaviourism in the *positive* sense, as a scientific method or habit of approach, is theologically quite neutral. It was, as it happens, pioneered by a declared atheist, J. B. Watson, and has been elaborated with considerable success by B. F. Skinner, who has also made little secret of his hostility to at least some aspects of Christian theology. Skinner's great contribution was to extend behavioural psychology beyond the conditioned-reflex analysis of behaviour, which had stemmed from Pavlov's success in training dogs to salivate when they heard a bell which had been associated with food. Skinner adopted what he called an 'operant' or 'instrumental' conditioning method, which is basically the same as that used by circus trainers to shape the behaviour of animals. Rather than imposing behaviour patterns by stimulation from outside, Skinner's method is to wait until the animal spontaneously does something that the trainer wants to happen, and then to reinforce this by rewarding it. So if you want a pigeon to peck consistently at a panel of a particular colour, you wait until he happens to peck at it, and then allow a food pellet to fall. If he pecks another colour he gets no pellet; so he comes gradually to peck the one that feeds him.

Although this is called instrumental or operant conditioning because the animal has to perform some operation in order to learn, one of the most interesting things about this method of shaping behaviour is that it can work without the trainee's knowledge. Moreover, it can work in men as well as in animals. (A few days after I told my schoolgirl daughters this, they came home in triumph and reported that their class had conspired successfully to condition their teacher to leave his rostrum and lecture from the far corner of the room. Their method was simply to look interested every time he moved to his left, and bored whenever he stood still or moved to his right!)

We shall look in the next chapter at the ethical implications of such techniques for shaping behaviour; but for the moment my point is that behaviourism as a scientific approach is only out to establish straightforward facts about the way we are constituted. We are so constituted that if a reward (a 'reinforcing stimulus') coincides sufficiently often with an action of ours, then we will become more likely to take that action in the future in similar circumstances; and I am suggesting that such 'behaviouristic' understanding of the way in which what we do is shaped by external influences is theologically neutral and not of itself at all inimical to human dignity, even though the application of it in particular situations might be (as we shall see later).

Negative behaviourism, however – behaviouristic *philosophy* as distinct from science – is anything but neutral. It is characterized by what it *denies*. In the writings of Skinner,[10] for example, it goes with the idea that concepts like 'freedom' or 'dignity' are 'pre-scientific' relics which are destined to be outdated by a scientific understanding of human behaviour purely in terms of conditioning, contingencies of reinforcement and the like. Religious values are downgraded to mere 'reinforcers' which are 'good' in Skinner's terms if they tend to favour survival. Freedom of choice is held to be an illusion based on ignorance of the psychological mechanisms involved in the shaping of behaviour; and so on.

How then should we react to all this if we wish to defend human dignity? First, it is vital to distinguish as clearly as possible between these positive and negative senses of 'behaviourism'. There is an understandable confusion between the two because the distinction is carefully avoided by writers like Skinner; and he has himself to thank for a good deal of the odium that his work has attracted among Christians and others anxious for the dignity of man. Every now and again he prints disclaimers of any reductionist intentions, but he fails to make the distinctions that would justify his self-defence. Secondly, as a corrective against unworthy fear, it would do no harm to remind ourselves positively to give thanks for whatever is true in what behavioural science has established, and cultivate an attitude of *hope* that we can go on discovering useful truth in this way about ourselves and our fellow human beings. Thirdly, there is a continuing need to expose remorselessly the fallacy of nothing-buttery on which negative behaviourism is based, showing the logical bankruptcy of this metaphysical parasite with respect to the scientific data whose respectability it tries to assume. Finally, those of us concerned to make constructive contributions to thought in this area must make special efforts to get accustomed to moving back and forth between the view in the scientific mirror and the Christian perspective on human behaviour, in such a way as to integrate the two. A recent book, *Psychology and Christianity – the view both ways*[11] by my friend Malcolm Jeeves, Professor of Psychology at St. Andrews, shows most helpfully what this means. There is no question of keeping a watertight compartment between the two; once you allow them to interrelate it becomes clear that they are entirely harmonious, and that the unity to which they bear witness is even more marvellous than anyone could realize from either view alone.

Determinism

Like behaviourism, the word 'determinism' has been used to express more than one idea. First, what we may by analogy call *positive* determinism stands for an innocent and theologically neutral scientific hypothesis: the speculation (essentially untestable) that for every event in the physical world there exist (even if you cannot find them) prior events which constitute sufficient causes of those events. 'No event without a physical cause.' As it stands, this is just a hypothesis about the kind of world God holds in being. It could be true, it could be false, without implying anything specifically religious or anti-religious. It expresses only a positive confidence in the reliability of scientific precedent as a guide to our future expectations. 'Determinism' is often used, however, in a *negative* sense to stand for a particular metaphysical doctrine, which denies human freedom and responsibility. Like negative behaviourism, negative determinism is often presented as if it had logical support from deterministic science; but as we shall see, this too is a bogus claim.

As it happens, since the German physicist Heisenberg enunciated his famous 'Uncertainty Principle' some fifty years ago, scientific (positive) determinism has fallen out of fashion. The reason is that if you try to use the equations of physics to predict the motions of the most minute particles such as electrons, you are bound to come unstuck. When an electron is released from the gun of a television tube, for example, Heisenberg showed that you could not predict from any prior observations, even in principle, the precise point at which it will strike the screen. We have to be content with statistical estimates, of the kind that insurance companies produce for things like mortality rates. In that sense, then, physics today is no longer deterministic; and it might seem natural for defenders of human dignity to accept this thankfully as a way of escape from negative (metaphysical) determinism.

To do so, however, would I think be a false move. In the first place, it would seem highly unwise to lay such emphasis on Heisenberg's Uncertainty Principle that if the fashion in physics were to swing in the next fifty years in some more deterministic direction, our defence of the dignity of man could come crumbling around our ears. Secondly, and more to the point, I do not believe that the kind of uncertainty expressed by Heisenberg's Principle is either necessary or appropriate for the defence of human responsibility.

At this point you might reasonably challenge me to explain in what sense one could ascribe responsibility to a human agent if – even if – physics had not gone indeterministic. Would not a physics that was deterministic (in the positive, technical sense) automatically lead to the doctrine we have called 'negative' determinism, that human responsibility is an illusion, and there is no such thing as a genuinely open choice? As this is a topic on which I have written elsewhere[12] recently,

I hope you will allow me to give here only a summary answer. Readers who want to skip can pick up the thread again on p. 55.

The standard argument of negative determinism is that if all the motions of your brain, and the rest of the universe around it, were fully determined by physical causes, then your whole future, including any future choices of yours, must already be inevitable before you make up your mind. Any impression you may have that the outcome depends on you must then be an illusion, based simply on ignorance of the physical details that determine your future.

At first this may sound like watertight logic. Generations of debaters, on both sides, have accepted it as a valid starting point, and have then striven to prove or disprove the hypothesis of *scientific* determinism, which is alleged to have these logical consequences. On closer examination, however, I believe we shall find a flaw in the logic of the standard argument itself – the argument accepted by both sides as a starting point. Once we see how big a hole this makes in the case for negative determinism, I believe we shall be left with no need, and no incentive, to take sides one way or the other on the purely scientific issue of the Uncertainty Principle.

The Flaw in the Classical Argument

The flaw in the classical argument arises from its use of the word 'inevitable'. Let us take it in stages. If all the motions of the universe, including your brain, were fully determined by physical causes, then (by definition) a super-intelligence who knew the complete state of the universe now could also in principle work out a complete specification of its future. So far, so good. (Note that we are not saying that our universe *is* like this, but only that if it *were* like this, the conclusion would follow.) But now comes the illegitimate logical jump in the classical argument. 'Therefore, your whole future, including all you think, believe or choose, must already be *inevitable*.' Where does this come from? The idea suggested is that if the future state of your brain were *predictable-by-a-super-intelligence*, it would then logically follow that it was *inevitable-for-you* – that there was nothing you could do about it. Plausible though this may sound, it turns out to be a quite invalid inference, for a logical reason which has nothing to do with any particular scientific theory of the way your brain works.

What do we mean by calling some future event 'inevitable'? A typical example would be the time of sunrise tomorrow. Given the assumptions of astronomy, this is something inevitable, in the sense that it must be reckoned with as stated, by *anyone* and *everyone*. Whether anyone knows it or not, or likes it or not, there exists a specification of the time of sunrise in a given locality which anyone and everyone would be correct to believe and mistaken to disbelieve. This specification, in other words, has an *unconditional claim* to the assent of all. It is the *unconditional* nature of this claim which makes sunrise at that time an *inevitable* (unavoidable) event for anyone and everyone. The same applies in general to all future events whose physical causes are independent (for practical purposes) of the physical state of human beings. If two massive bodies in interstellar space were to collide, for instance, an astronomer might describe this as 'inevitable'. It would not matter whether anyone actually had calculated their time of collision. It would be enough for him to prove that before the event *there existed in principle* a detailed specification of the time (and outcome) which had an unconditional claim to the assent of anyone and everyone. If only they had known it, they would have been correct to believe it and in error to disbelieve it, whether they liked it or not. Its claim was binding upon everyone, whether they knew it or not.

In all such cases, there could of course be no question of our accepting *responsibility* for the events in question. 'It had nothing to do with me, I was only a helpless spectator. What I might have thought, decided or done could have made no difference. It was inevitable-for-me, unavoidable-by-me.' In saying this, we are not suggesting that no alternative outcome was *logically* possible. Nothing could rule out the logical possibility of an event that broke completely with scientific precedent. We mean only that whatever the basis for the future specification, *our* assent or dissent, our action or inactivity, were not among the factors determining its correctness or otherwise. Its claim to our assent was *unconditional*.

When we turn to consider the future states of your brain, however, the situation is strikingly different. Suppose (just for the sake of argument) that your brain were as mechanistic in its operations as the solar system. You might then imagine that the state it will be in tomorrow would be as inevitable for you as the position of the sun at the same time. In other words, you might imagine that there must exist (though of course unknown to you) a detailed specification of the entire future state of your brain which has an unconditional logical claim to your assent here and now, if only you knew it. Oddly enough, this would not follow. Why not? The answer is really quite simple. The big and quite fundamental difference between the *sunrise* tomorrow and the *state of your brain* tomorrow is that whereas the physical course of the sun is quite independent of what you choose to think about it or anything else, the detailed physical state of your brain is *not* independent of what you choose to think. On the contrary, the assumption of mechanistic brain science is that all you think, believe, hope, experience, and so on is represented by the physical state of some part of your brain, in something of the sense in which the equation that a computer is solving is represented by the detailed physical state of the computer. It follows from that assumption that there must be one part of your brain – namely the mechanism that represents *what you believe* – which must necessarily *change* if any change takes place in what you believe.

Does there then exist now a complete specification of *that* part of your brain, which you would be both correct to believe and mistaken to disbelieve if only you knew it? Obviously not. Suppose I had the means of analyzing your brain state and producing a complete description of it which is correct as I see it here and now; then obviously if you were to believe it, *that state must change*. By the same token, even if I could calculate completely the immediate future of your brain from my description (without letting you know), my detailed prediction would have no claim to *your* assent. What *I* would be correct (secretly) to believe about your future is something that *you* would be *mistaken* to believe!

Notice the element of *relativity* here. It is not that you are simply *ignorant of the truth* about your future, as if what I would be correct to believe was what you would be correct to believe if only you knew it. On the contrary, what I believe is something on which you and I would be mistaken to agree, because *I* would be mistaken to believe it if you believed it. With respect to your detailed future brain states, you and I must believe differently in order that each of us should believe correctly. For the immediate future of your brain, *there does not exist* a completely detailed description which you and I would both be correct to accept as inevitable. The future-tense detailed description that would be accurate-for-me is necessarily inaccurate-for-you (until after the event), and in that sense cannot claim beforehand to be the *truth for you*. In retrospect you may be able to agree that it was accurate-for-me, and that it stands as an accurate description of what later took place, but it would still be clear to both of us that it had no claim to your assent before the time in question. For you, the detailed future of your brain must be (in that sense) *indeterminate*, even though its processes were physically-determinate. This does not mean only that you cannot *discover* what its future will be. It means that its future *has no fully-determinate detailed specification for you to discover*, with an unconditional claim to your assent.

At this point you may feel that I have been neglecting an obvious possibility. Why, you may ask, can we not allow for the effect of your believing my description on the state of your brain, so as to calculate a description which would become accurate if you were to believe it? For certain technical reasons, this may not be possible; but to test the weight of the objection, suppose it were. Suppose I could cook up a description of your brain which would become accurate provided you believed it. What then? It is now a description which at the moment is false, because of course it will become accurate only if you believe it. It has therefore no claim to an observer's assent. Moreover, even though *you* would be correct to believe it, you would not be in error to *disbelieve* it, because as it stands it is false. Since what you are not believing is something which at the moment is false, you cannot be held to be 'under an illusion'. Oddly enough, then, the fact is that in a strict sense the accuracy of my cooked-up description *depends on you*. If you believed it, it would be accurate. If you disbelieved it, it would be false. Unlike predictions of future sunrises it has, and can have, no fixed and determinate truth-status independent of what you think or decide. On the contrary, *you* are the determinant of its truth or falsehood, for which therefore you cannot escape (or be denied) responsibility, even if your brain processes were fully determinate in a physical sense.

Notice that we are not denying that our imaginary super-scientist could predict whether or not you would believe his prediction if offered to you. What we are discussing is the *logical status* of his prediction – the logical strength of its claim to universal assent – whether or not you actually accept it, and especially in the normal situation where you never even get to hear of it. What our argument proves is that even if a super-scientist could have the kind of knowledge we have imagined, the most that brain science could produce (even in principle) is a specification of the future of your brain whose accuracy in detail is *up to you*, and whose logical claim to your assent beforehand depends strictly upon what you think about it.

Note also that we have made no assumptions here about your being 'counter-suggestible' or perverse in your attitude towards the imaginary superscientist. It is true, as I argued in an early paper,[13] that if a superscientist were to try to persuade you that it was inevitable for you to choose, say, porridge rather than prunes for breakfast, you could indefinitely frustrate him. But this is only an illustration, and not a demonstration, of the logical point. The central argument applies even in cases where no communication is made with the person in question.

You will I hope have realized that our objective here has been strictly limited. We have not attempted to spell out all the necessary and sufficient conditions for human responsibility, still less to prove that these conditions hold in all cases. All I have claimed is that one particular kind of attack on human dignity – the denial of responsibility on the basis of the (assumed) physical determinateness of the brain – is based on a logical mistake. The *positive* scientific theory that all physical events are determined by physical causes does not logically imply the *negative* metaphysical belief that the immediate future of a human agent is inevitable for him. The same holds good for theories of the determination of behaviour by genetic or psychological causes (and, I might add, for theological theories of the determination of behaviour by theological causes). None of them logically implies that the outcome of my choosing is inevitable for me before I make up my mind. Predictability-for-detached-non-participants does *not* necessarily imply inevitability-for-the-agents-involved.

You will see now, I hope, why I urged defenders of human dignity not to try to prove that responsible human actions are unpredictable-in-principle for non-participant observers. They may well be so: indeed if Heisenberg's Principle is correct, all events in the physical world are unpredictable in full detail; and as we saw in Chapter 2, any idea of completely predicting the future of a human brain is hopelessly unrealistic. But what we must avoid is the suggestion that responsibility for an action *requires* it to have been unpredictable-for-others: that the predictability of an action by observers would be a sufficient ground for denying responsibility for it. It is this suggestion, and not deterministic brain science or psychology as such, that must be exposed and resisted as the real enemy of human dignity.

In order to deny a man the dignity of being held responsible for a decision (good or bad), the negative determinist would have to show that the outcome was *inevitable-for-him*; and this, as we have seen, can be frustrated in an important class of cases without invoking Heisenberg's Principle or any other weakening of physical causality in the brain.

Conclusion

What I have been saying throughout this and the previous chapter, in a number of ways, amounts to this: When you find someone trying to debunk human dignity in the name of science, it is important not to be misled into attacking his science instead of attacking the faulty philosophy which invariably underlies attacks of that kind. By all means, if you do find flaws in his science, point them out as a matter of brotherly kindness to a scientist, just as you would point out a flaw in a tyre as a matter of kindness to a motorist. But do not imagine that the way to defend human dignity is to attack his science as such; for by doing so you would merely compound his confusion. It is the faulty philosophy of the debunkers that should be our target. Above all, those who claim to serve the God of Truth must remember that our duty is to be obedient to all data, not merely because he is monitoring our honesty, but because he is the Giver of those data. Those who love him owe it to him to respond in glad obedience, rather than grudging or fearful capitulation, to all he allows us to learn about our marvellous and mysterious embodiment.

CHAPTER 4

Responsibility for the Future

Human Engineering

When you hear the words 'human engineering', I wonder what you think of. Aldous Huxley's *Brave New World*? The stockbreeding of a race of morons to serve as the slaves of their scientific masters? Brainwashing or mind control by cynical political tyrants? For several generations now the science fiction writers have had their fling on topics such as these. In the earlier days there was a good deal of euphoria. Man, pictured as the crown of the evolutionary process, was set fair for perfectibility by his own efforts. Science was to bring him release from the limitations that he inherited from his primitive ancestry, and incidentally religion would, of course, wither away as a superfluous relic. More recently, jarring notes of pessimism have spoilt the harmony of this chorus in our own honour. Having seen some samples of what scientific technology can do to destroy the human environment and enslave the human mind, many of our fellow earthlings have turned in revulsion from the discredited idol of scientism; and they abhor above all the idea of applying science to the shaping of the future of man himself.

How far is this attitude justifiable? At first sight it might seem the obvious way of humility. Is not contentment after all one of the hallmarks of the truly human being, and of the Christian not least? Is it not arrogant to want to change the way God makes people? What right has man to play God? – a question posed by many people in our day, both Christians and non-Christians (the latter of course using the term 'God' in decent quotation marks). In any case, is not the idea of human perfectibility basically heretical from the standpoint of biblical Christianity?

I do not deny that proper concerns lie behind such questions; but the general attitude they express is, I fear, a false humility. It is more akin to the pagan fear of nature, which I think our civilization has inherited from the ancient Greeks, than to the fear of God in the positive sense that the Bible gives to that phrase. The first question suggests a confusion between *contentment with the unalterable*, which is indeed a Christian virtue, and *complacency in face of the alterable*, which can be a rejection of one aspect of our human responsibility and dignity. There is no biblical warrant whatsoever for complacency in the face of alterable circumstances which are recognizably bad. 'He that knoweth to do good and doeth it not, to him it is sin,' says the proverb; and this teaching runs throughout the Bible, indicating that although there is indeed a sense in which everybody and everything owes its being to God as Creator, it is simply bad theology to conclude from this that God places an embargo on taking our share of responsibility for the way things turn out next. There is no evidence that this is less true of the genetic balance of the human population than of other aspects of our daily activities. So far from its being arrogant for the Christian to want to eliminate genetic defects, then, it may in fact be a duty.

The distinction we need here is between *creation* (which is God's prerogative) and *procreation* (which is man's responsibility). 'Creation' refers to that eternal (extra-temporal) generative act of God through which our world is given its being – the *fiat* by virtue of which there is anything at all in our world. Procreation on the other hand is the process within our created spacetime by which human beings bring other human beings into the world. They do so according to a pattern that they only dimly understand, whether at the level of its biological mechanism or of its statistical consequences. The pattern is in an ultimate sense God's pattern; but it is not so in a sense that would absolve them from all responsibility for the way that pattern works out statistically. Here indeed we have the theological counterpart of the argument sketched at the end of Chapter 3. The sovereignty of God does not at all imply that every aspect of the future is inevitable-for-us. On the contrary, the biblical doctrine is that we are accountable to our Creator for those decisions and actions that are up to us, precisely because he has made us the determinants of them. As we saw in Chapter 3, our being the determinants of our actions does not require those actions to be unpredictable to non-participants.

This makes explicit the mistake in asking what right man has to 'play God'. Undertaken in the proper spirit, human engineering is not *playing* God at all, but *serving* God. playing the man if you like; but not playing God. Fortunately for us, *that* is impossible in principle.

But, you may ask, is not the idea of human perfectibility indeed heretical, at least in Christian theology? If we take 'perfectibility' literally, of course the Christian answer is yes. Human perfectibility by human effort is impossible; the grace of God is quite essential if man is ever to reach perfection. But this surely is not the issue. What concerns us in human engineering is not perfectibility at all; it is something much more modest which we might call *improvability*. And the idea of human improvability, so far from being heretical, is something the Christian must examine as a matter of duty. Is it possible to improve the human lot, to strengthen the human constitution, as judged by standards which are compatible with those of the Bible? This question, I suggest, can be answered only by looking to see. There is no sin in seeking to mitigate the effects of our fallenness as human beings.

Perhaps I may quote here from a statement issued after a conference on *Human Engineering and the Future of Man*,[14] held under Christian auspices in 1975 at Wheaton College in the United States: 'Jesus summed up man's responsibility in two commands – to love God with all one's being, and to love one's neighbour as oneself. Christians recognize in this second command the responsibility to do all they can to alleviate the host of evils and suffering which entered the world through the fall of man. Among the many accomplishments of science, certain techniques of genetic, neurological and psychological modification of man have great potential either to enhance or to erode his capacity to serve God and neighbour. Because man is both finite and sinful, restraints upon his application of the tools of technology are needed. In particular, care must be taken to preserve the freedom, dignity and spiritual responsibility of man who is created in the image of God.' So far from this area being one from which Christians must shy away with hands raised in holy horror, then, I believe we ought to see the potentialities of human engineering as a challenge to the compassionate exercise of Christian obedience. It is not indeed a challenge to be met in any easy or simple way; but it is one put squarely before us by the same God who has empowered us to discover the data that give us the responsibility.

What sort of guide-lines should we keep in mind in entering on this responsibility, and trying to be positive in our obedience? At the level of motivation, there are two strands to which I have already referred. The first is compassion. We must test any proposal in this general area, where we try to take practical responsibility for the future of our fellow men, by this criterion: asking whether it would exhibit realistic love to God and our fellow man. The second strand in our motivation must be what the Bible terms the fear of God: 'fear' here being the kind of loving, reverent, cautious but eager obedience that a son shows towards his father in an ideal family relationship; or, to put it in another context, the fear of the steward whose master will hold him answerable for the use he has made of what he has been given. We remember the parable of the talents, and the image of the poor cringing wretch who had been given one talent, but kept it wrapped up in a napkin rather than make any use of it, on the grounds that his master was 'a hard man'. Because he was scared that anything he did would bring disapproval he did nothing – which was the worst course of all. The accusation of which we would have a right to be afraid on the Day of Judgement is this: 'You knew what good could be done in this way or that, and you did nothing.' Knowledge, then, brings inescapable responsibility. The question before us is not whether, but how, we should apply it.

Secondly, having emphasized that we must test our ambitions here by the criterion of compassion, it is important for us to distinguish *compassion* for others from what might be called *ambition* for others. By ambition for others I mean setting a target which may have a superficial desirability on compassionate grounds, but which may also involve undue risks, or may involve stretching the individual beyond what he can happily encompass. When we become ambitious for him rather than ambitious simply to serve him, he becomes, as it were, a vicarious vehicle of our ambition for ourselves. This is a real danger. We see for example a community of native tribesmen, and our compassion moves us to wish that they could have the benefits of education and whatever else modern science makes possible for them. So far, perhaps, so good – though even there it might be incumbent on us to work out what in practice is likely to be the outcome of our compassionate plans to educate them according to our Western standards. The danger is that we then move to the second phase, where we take the kind of attitude that, say, a greyhound owner takes to the racing abilities of his dog. We become ambitious for those whom we are trying to educate and train up, and we put them through a routine in which real compassion, 'feeling with' them what it is like to be them, fades out, and our ambition for them becomes a menace to their real welfare.

Thirdly under the heading of guide-lines, I suggest that we have to make *answerability* our constant watchword. This is a theme to which we will return. In any attempt to serve our fellow men, and above all where our attempt is based on the 'spectator attitude' of science, it is crucial that we should desire to be accountable as far as possible both to God and to our fellow men, for the exercises on which we embark and for the ambitions and hopes and schemes that we entertain. If this thought should ever begin to irk us, we have gone beyond our brief.

Finally, in an area of this sort where our ignorance is so much greater than our knowledge, it is essential that we proceed both slowly and if possible reversibly, so that we can undo what we have tried to do if there are signs that it is going wrong. In any aspect of human nature, whether genetic or physiological or psychological or social, we are dealing with a self-regulating system of such exquisite complexity that to touch even one of the controls could have effects like those of the proverbial bull in a china shop. We are dealing with a situation where we may have no way of knowing in advance what disasters could be triggered by well intentioned moves. Please God as our science grows we may be able to foresee more and more of the snags; but it will never be possible for us to relax into a reckless or carefree mood in which we can go straight ahead without fear of unexpected consequences. We have to remember always that the suffering products of our experiments will be fellow human beings who – like the thalidomide children – will be stuck with the result for the rest of their lives.

With these principles in mind, then, I want to look at a couple of practical examples of the responsibility that human science imposes on us in the sight of God towards our fellow men. We are not now asking what our scientific understanding does in theory to our image of man; we are asking what it does in practice to our responsibility for the future of our fellow men.

Genetic Engineering

As our first example let us take what is sometimes called 'genetic engineering'. You may be relieved to know that I will not be going deeply into technical details, because this is not my own scientific field. My object is mainly to ask what kinds of issue are raised, particularly for Christians, by the possibility of shaping the genetic composition of the human population.

Just a little of the scientific background may help us put the question into perspective. The key to modern genetics has been the discovery of the so-called DNA molecule. In man each of these is composed of an immense chain of about 3,000 million pairs of small unit molecules called nucleotides. In each species these units are strung together in a definite order, characteristic of the species. Just as the different messages on the pages of a book are spelt out by different selections from a small alphabet, so the units in the DNA molecules function as code symbols in messages that tell the dividing cells in an embryo what proteins (structural building bricks) to produce at which points. These nucleotide units, the 'letters' of the DNA 'alphabet', are of only four different sorts. The same four sorts are found in all the cells of all living creatures. They differ only in their order and their total number; and they function in groups of which everyone has heard, called *genes*. An average gene may be made up of about a thousand of these units. The genes, like the words in a book, are strung together to form a long very complex structure in a certain definite order; and in a normal human cell there are 46 volumes of these words, each volume being called a *chromosome*. It is only the variations in the number and order of the units in the string that determine whether the body that is produced will be that of a plant, a fish, a human genius or a human idiot. Each of the thousand billion cells that make up a normal human body has the same 46 volumes of instructions for building a complete human being. The process by which the building instructions are divided and shared out and reassembled when a sperm is united with an egg turns out to be subject to a good deal of uncontrolled variation. For example, it is believed that at least one in five human embryos conceived may have the wrong number of 'volumes' in their cells. They may have 45 or 47 chromosomes instead of 46. As it happens, most of these perish *in utero*; the misprinted instructions simply fail to produce a viable organism. Consequently most human individuals have in fact 46 chromosomes; but variations in the make-up of these chromosomes can be enormous, and such variations are believed to be responsible for all the differences between the inborn characteristics of different human beings: their physical powers, their resistance or proneness to diseases, their basic intelligence and so forth.

One particular genetic abnormality, where there is an extra 'Y' chromosome, has become notorious. Typically, out of every 1,000 male adults, two or three may be of this 'XYY' type. It has been found that an abnormally large proportion of these turn up in hospitals for the criminally insane, though it seems that others may lead well-adjusted lives.[15]

Needless to say, I am not here denying that environmental factors such as diet, training and exercise (both physical and intellectual) also play a crucial role in human development. Recent attempts to play down the respective roles of 'heredity' or 'environment' (according to political taste) have been a disgrace to the objectivity of science, and it is to be hoped that Christians at least will be fearlessly honest in keeping the record straight in future, however unpopular this may be. But the question that concerns us here is at a different level. What kind of responsibility does this growing knowledge lay upon us, if we are true humanists, concerned for the maximal fulfilment of the potential of our fellow human beings? Let me mention briefly three possibilities by way of illustration.

First, by examining the contents of the genetic 'library' in cells cast off from a developing embryo in the uterus, it is already to some extent possible to detect genetic defects that might otherwise result in the development of a seriously handicapped child. The process, called amniocentesis, involves the extraction of a small amount of liquid from the uterus so that cells cast off from the embryo can be cultured for examination. It is thus possible to warn a mother at an early stage that the developing embryo will produce (for example) a mongol child if it is allowed to go to term. The same method incidentally allows the sex of the embryo to be determined. Now of course all this raises a huge additional moral question, as to which kinds of defect, if any, would justify abortion of the embryo. Many people, whether Christian or not, would find something repugnant in the idea that if parents wanted a boy rather than a girl, they should be given the information and the means to destroy a perfectly healthy embryo merely because it turns out to be of the wrong sex. Where serious defects are diagnosed, however, the moral issues are more complex. I do not suggest that such questions have an answer ready-made in the Bible or anywhere else; and it would certainly be too simplistic to dismiss them merely by quoting the Sixth Commandment. But I think it vital that Christians seek to bring biblical priorities, and not merely pragmatic considerations, to bear on the effort to answer them wisely.

A second possibility with startling implications is that of 'repairing' defective genes. Could chemical engineering allow the biologist, once he has discovered that one of the genes contributed by a parent is defective, to replace the defective group of symbols by one which is known to produce a normal child? According to Dr. Robert Sinsheimer of California Institute of Technology,[16] one of the leaders in the field, this is a far distant prospect as far as man is concerned. There are indications from 'recombinant DNA' research that it is possible at a very lowly level in the animal kingdom to substitute genes; and in that sense some repair of genetic inheritance is feasible. As applied to men, however, the authorities in the field seem to regard it very much as science fiction.

There is however a third possibility which is much more likely; indeed it is already with us. This is the use of mass screening of potential parents in order to detect any defective genes before damage is done. Parents could voluntarily have their genetic 'library' analyzed scientifically to see whether if they had a child it would be likely to suffer for example from sickle-cell anaemia or other crippling diseases. On this basis it would then be possible for people voluntarily at least to refrain from increasing the number of children suffering from these diseases. Of course it is obvious that in a sufficiently dictatorial society such discipline might be imposed on people; and to that extent it might be considered a threat to human dignity. But it is true of almost any scientific development, alas, that it could be unethically abused by a dictator; and the risk of this does not seem to me to justify turning our backs on the prospect of improving the health of the next generation by what we might call 'stock weeding', as opposed to 'stock breeding'.

Even the voluntary screening of potential parents, of course, raises many sensitive issues. If you wanted to be unsympathetic you might call it 'genetic branding'. Should the possession of a seriously defective gene be made legally notifiable, like infection with a dangerous disease? How much knowledge should be fed back to the individual concerned, and in which cases? There will after all be a lot of awkward borderlines. Suppose for example that it were possible one day to identify genes for colour-blindness, or tone-deafness, or other minor disabilities. It would be a moot point whether somebody who submitted to test and was found likely to produce a colour-blind child should be bothered with such information.

But although one can foresee very difficult practical problems I would suggest that these are really no different from other awkward borderline problems that we have had to learn to live with. (For example, at what stage do you turn off the respirator of a brain-damaged patient? If there is only one kidney machine available and ten people waiting for it, who shall have it?) It would be difficult to argue that problems of this kind could justify giving up the foreseeable benefits.

In contradistinction to 'stock weeding' of this kind, there have also been proposals for large scale stock *breeding* of human beings. There are at least two different forms that human stock breeding could take. The first, which has of course been practised on a small scale over many generations, achieves its aim by encouraging or permitting only selected strains of individual to procreate. Royalty for example have long tended to stock-breed, and many other strata of society in different parts of the world have accepted or enjoined the custom of selecting the mates that their daughters or sons were allowed to marry. Of course if this were to be done on a scientific basis then all kinds of undesirable complications can be envisaged; but it is at any rate something which would involve, in principle, a minimum of interference with the normal pattern of human reproduction by comparison with the other possibility, which is called *cloning*.

Cloning

Cloning means essentially developing a large number of identical individuals from a single cell, and so avoiding the hazard of allowing husband and wife to shuffle their genes in the union of sperm and egg. It does not need much imagination to foresee the complex social and personal problems that would arise if cloning of human beings became general. Admittedly, according to the experts, the cloning of man is a very long way off; but that does not excuse us from asking what issues the possibility raises. It is in this area that the dangers of ignorantly tampering with a complex mechanism are particularly serious. The point is that the genetic ecosystem, by which I mean the whole world of plants, animals and men in which genes are represented, has hitherto been self-regulating. It has developed a most intricate structure of checks and balances that presumably maintain some sort of dynamic equilibrium which has been in existence for many thousands of years. With such an immensely complex system, involving interactions between a whole range of genetic 'libraries' each of which comprises thousands of millions of symbols, it must clearly be impossible in principle to foresee the outcome of all but the simplest changes. To take just one example (not involving cloning), it is certainly possible now for the sex of a human embryo to be determined at a very early stage and in principle (whatever we think of the moral implications) for it to be aborted if the parents want a child of the opposite sex. What would it do to the population dynamics of our society if it were possible for all parents to opt for the sex of child they wanted? Might the system go into a wild oscillation, where you would have far too many men in the first generation, far too many women in the next and so on? What would be the social byproducts of a gross imbalance between the sexes? Would they be *good* for mankind? We are dealing with a delicately balanced mechanism millions of times more complex than a radio or a wrist watch or even a computer; so caution here is not a sign of failure of nerve. To quote again Professor Sinsheimer:[16] 'Whenever man intervenes to alter a balance provided by nature then man must establish his own balance, his own checks and controls, his own constraints. And thus in seeking to enlarge human freedom we must be careful that we do not in fact diminish it.'

Some Christians might feel that in warning against these dangers I am not going at all far enough. A recent writer in a Christian periodical, for example, expressed fears lest genetic means of altering or improving life 'imply a casual attitude towards an easily rearranged set of genes and chromosomes', against which the Christian must object. Efforts of this kind were castigated as 'the reduction of life to matter alone'. Now it may at first sound very proper for a Christian to talk in these terms and to insist (as this particular writer did) that 'humans must not be reduced to objects of scientific experimentation'. But is such a negative response a realistic interpretation of our Christian duty? I am bound to say that despite their excellent intentions, arguments of this kind (of which there are many about) seem to express just the attitude against which I want to warn Christian defenders of human dignity.

To presuppose, for example, that a mechanistic approach to the elimination of genetically-determined deformity 'reduces human life to matter alone' is to commit the same fallacy as the opponents of human dignity. There is no biblical warrant at all for declaring the human body, as an object, exempt from scientific experimentation. Obviously the possible *cost* to the individual must be considered when deciding whether a given experiment is justified; but that is another matter. Most of the advances in medicine for which we are thankful today have perforce been developed as a result of experimental tests on sick people. It could show the very reverse of true compassion to lay down as a rule that human beings must not be allowed to be objects of scientific experimentation. In all such matters we must take care to have our sights realistically on the well-being of our fellow men, and avoid the dangers of slogan-ridden thinking. 'Sacredness of personality', 'sacredness of life' and the like may sound good guides; but in practice we can use them only under the overall control of compassion: a practical compassion that is determined not to miss an opportunity of doing good merely because it may be unpopular or unconventional.

To take another example, there has been a good deal of argument against cloning, not because it might be abused but on the grounds that the very idea of reproducing a number of identical human beings would 'destroy human individuality and human dignity'. Once again, the intention is admirable; but let us test the logic. Consider again our friend John Smith, who leads his dignified existence in a small rural community. If I tell you that John Smith has an identical twin brother, does this do any damage to his individuality? Merely to ask the question reveals the fallacy. What distinguishes a man as a human individual is basically the unique pattern of *roles* and *relationships* he bears among his fellows, and not any necessary dissimilarity of his body from theirs. To this distinctiveness the number of John Smith's brothers, and the extent to which they are biologically 'identical' with him, are totally irrelevant. The problems posed by having a biologically 'identical' twin are not ontological (i.e. they do not affect the essence or personal identity of the individual) but merely practical – the need to wear distinctive clothing, answer to different names and the like. At the microscopic level of their nervous systems, of course, the term 'identical' is a misnomer.

Such twins are no more identical than two computers of the same design which have acquired different programmes and different stores of information. However similar the nervous systems of twins may have been at an early stage, the differences in their detailed experience, especially in their individual human relationships, will have rapidly transformed the internal structure of each into something totally unique and distinctive, giving rise to differences of 'conditional readiness' beside which any external resemblances are quite trivial. Each is a fully unique individual; each plays his role in his local community with individual dignity, to which the existence of his 'identical' brother makes not a whit of difference. Emotional reactions to the idea of cloning, based on the theory that it would destroy individuality and dignity, are in fact a menace to the true basis of human dignity; for however well-intentioned, they only deflect attention from the role-playing uniqueness that really matters.

This said, there are of course other and much more solid objections to the use of cloning to multiply human beings. Perhaps the most serious is the risk that such people would be deprived of the delicate pattern of parent-child relationships on which normal psychological development depends. For this and other reasons I am far from advocating human cloning as a desirable use of scientific resources. What I am suggesting is that it would be inept to try to hang our objections to it on the peg of 'human dignity'. It is not in their claim to respect as individuals, but in their quality of life, that cloned human beings might be seriously and pitiably deficient.

The Shaping of Behaviour

Genetic engineering has occupied what you might consider a disproportionate amount of this chapter, especially as its practical impact may still be far in the future; but I believe that a great deal of damage is done to our image of man by fear of what might come in the future, based on false presuppositions about the basis of human dignity. I shall deal more briefly with our second example, which is the shaping of behaviour. We have already looked at some of the scientific background when we considered behavioural analysis, typified by B. F. Skinner's technology for circus training of animals and human beings, the shaping of behaviour by reward and punishment. What issues does this raise when applied practically?

First let us be clear that there is nothing new about it in principle. "Train up a child in the way in which he should go, and when he is old he will not depart from it."[17] We have good biblical warrant for the shaping of behaviour, and for the expectation that the result can be reliable. What is new, of course, is that we know a little more now about the processes by which we can encourage or discourage particular sorts of behaviour. I wish we knew more. The literature (particularly of educational psychology) sometimes suggests that we know far more than we do. Nevertheless our knowledge is growing; and I suggest that if we apply it humanely to 'train up a child in the way wherein he should go' we are doing nothing whatever contrary to the biblical injunction.

Why then do we so often have the feeling that there is something demeaning, something sneaky, something unfair about behavioural manipulation? Is there not something here that we ought (whether we are Christian or not) to be restive about? I think there is. I think there is a kind of behavioural manipulation which is quite unacceptable, for reasons which are unemotional and objective, in the sense that they can be appraised coolly and evaluated rationally. We shall come to these in a moment, but let me start with some negatives. As with genetic engineering, it is easy in our enthusiasm for human dignity to make false moves in opposing behavioural manipulation. I believe that the kind of manipulation that is unacceptable is so *not* because all manipulation as such is wrong, *nor* because it involves a behaviouristic approach to human beings, *nor* because it makes people's behaviour more predictable. Let us take each of these in turn.

In manipulation, one individual has a large say in deciding how to shape another, who may not even be consulted. This can be perfectly ethical, and indeed obligatory. All of us start as infants by being manipulated. We are not asked for our opinions when first nappies are pinned on and various other things are done to us. Manipulation as such, dealing with an individual as an object, is not wrong. Even depersonalized manipulation may be obligatory. The surgeon deals with me on the operating table as a depersonalized object. It is his job. Depersonalization in that sense is not wrong as such.

Secondly, as we saw in the last chapter, there is nothing wrong with a behaviouristic approach as such. To treat it as something inseparable from an atheistic view of man is a mistake. Even if a behavioural analysis were *exhaustive* at its own level, it is not at all *exclusive* of other levels. A behaviouristic approach to the improvement of school teaching methods, for example, may ignore many humanly important aspects of the life of the pupils. But this of course is simply a consequence of the focusing power of the scientific lens or mirror, and does not in the least deny the validity and importance of these other aspects, nor excuse any neglect of them.

Thirdly, there is nothing necessarily inimical to human dignity in the possibility of predicting people's behaviour, once we realize that this does not of itself abolish their responsibility for the actions concerned (see Chapter 3).

What kind of manipulation is it, then, that is objectionable? The key question, I suggest, is how far in principle the manipulator is or wants to be *answerable* to the person he is manipulating. Any contrived way of handling our fellow men that destroys or evades the answerability of the manipulator to the manipulated person is unacceptable. Why is answerability so important? Consider what happens when two people are fully open to one another in dialogue. Viewed from a scientific standpoint, each can be regarded as an information-system which is *interlocked* with the other. Each is vulnerable to the address of the other in such a way that some lines of cause-and-effect form closed loops that run through each into the other and back again. That is what gives the experience of dialogue its unique quality. In a clear technical sense, each participant system *interpenetrates* the other.

Now you will remember from the last chapter that the immediate future of a human agent is necessarily indeterminate in a certain sense, until he makes up his mind what it shall be. By the same reasoning it follows that when two people become one system in dialogue, each is to some extent indeterminate for the other as well as for himself. This 'mutual indeterminacy' is an essential ingredient in the respect we feel for one another. If however you were to adopt a relationship to another human being which cut completely the possibility of forming such closed loops, then the other would become a mere object to you, in principle fully specifiable. In that one-way relationship he cannot fulfil his role as 'thou' to you: the I-thou relation between you and him is impossible. In special circumstances, as in a surgical operating theatre, there need of course be no breach of the *spirit* of dialogue. You simply say good-bye to the surgeon until he has finished manipulating you, and then you are back and he is glad to be answerable to you. But the objectionable manipulator is the individual who in effect installs a one-way screen out of a desire to keep himself invulnerable from you while leaving you vulnerable to him. He does not *wish* to be answerable. It is the *one-way*, 'thing-making' character of the relationship which is basically objectionable in the kind of behavioural shaping that we should resist in the name of human dignity.

So a humane educator, for example, may be teaching very small children with whom he cannot have a fully symmetrical dialogue; but in principle he cherishes his answerability to them. He will be glad if in later years they come and ask him why he manipulated them as he did. He is undeniably a manipulator in the technical sense that he exerts a shaping influence over which they have no control; but the spirit in which he manipulates does not break the essential relationship of dialogue. He is still *potentially answerable*.

This throws some objective light on the distinction between ethical educational methods and unethical indoctrination. The indoctrinator in the bad sense is the individual who desires to prevent from developing between him and his victims the kind of reciprocal relationship in which he would be as vulnerable to their address (especially their questions) as they are vulnerable to his. The indoctrinator seeks only to impose, and rejects the relationship in which each is indeterminate for the other.

You may feel inclined to object that if infants are so young that dialogue is impossible, this does not seem a very practical distinction. But in fact we can make it practical for each one of us quite easily by a kind of thought experiment. What I must do is to ask myself, whenever I am in this position, how I would respond if a mature 'advocate' of the child came alongside me now and questioned me on his behalf. This, though it is only a thought experiment, is a deep-going test; indeed for those of us who are Christians it is clear that there is such an advocate. When Christ said, 'Inasmuch as you did it (or did it not) to the least of these, you did it (or did it not) to me', he made it clear that *he* stands as the universal Advocate for all those among our fellow men with whom we have to do. For the Christian at least, then, this is a thought experiment not merely in the sense of idle imagination. This is daily work; this is what prayer, in that context, would be all about – a test of our motivation by exposing it to Christ, and asking him to put his finger on anything unworthy. So the notion of potential answerability, if we take it seriously, cuts through all kinds of humbug, and liberates us in principle to use our growing behavioural knowledge to the full for the benefit of the next generation, in education and in other areas.

You may feel inclined to protest that you would still rather have nothing to do with the shaping of human behaviour; but in fact this is not a real option. Behavioural shaping is what we are doing to one another, willy nilly, all the time. The only choice is between doing it knowingly and doing it unknowingly. Because our nervous system is to some extent 'plastic', especially in early life, such mutual shaping is actually a necessity if we are to develop and maintain a normal healthy human personality. All of us depend from earliest infancy on psychological influences and interactions that would be manipulative if they were exercised deliberately. In recent years there has been growing evidence, both psychological and physiological, that unless the developing nervous system is exposed at the right stage to the right diet of inputs, its owner may never develop normal abilities to perceive and communicate. It is equally important to have early and consistent feedback from fellow human beings to enable a healthy priority scheme to develop. Since we depend on others for all of this, it would show the reverse of compassion if they were to deny us the shaping we need. This applies both to the upbringing of children and to the adult process that we call socialization.

As long as we do these things unthinkingly and unscientifically our consciences are curiously at rest. It is only when our attention is drawn to what we are doing from a scientific standpoint that we begin to feel uneasy. The danger then is that we may slide in one of two opposite directions. On the one hand there are many people today who react with horror. 'Who am I,' they say, 'to impose my views on my children? I must do my best to avoid conditioning them, and to let them make up their own minds on everything.' As a result, their offspring grow up deprived of much of the early 'programming' necessary for healthy normal development. The opposite reaction, perhaps less common, is to rush for all the latest textbooks on behavioural manipulation, adopt a depersonalized calculating attitude, and design home life inhumanly around mechanical 'schedules of reinforcement'. Both of these extremes, I suggest, violate human dignity by denying the rights and needs of the young people to whom we are potentially answerable. Both, incidentally, violate also the pattern of family relationships that we find sketched in the Bible as God's intention for man: the ideal environment for the growing personality, in which both aspects blend harmoniously.

Brainwashing

At this point let me refer briefly to 'brainwashing'. The term is often colloquially used to refer to any form of propaganda or even straightforward instruction of a kind disliked by the speaker. This is misleading. Strictly, as William Sargent has made clear in his instructive (if sometimes tendentious) book *Battle for the Mind*,[18] brainwashing means the use of psychological or physiological violence to destroy the critical faculties of the victim, inducing a pathological readiness to accept beliefs without adequate evidence.

When the violence involves overt cruelty (as in the notorious brainwashing procedures of some autocratic régimes) the unethical element seems obvious. Where it does not (as for example when the brainwasher simply works up excitement that may be felt as pleasurable) it may be less easy to see what is unethical about it. My suggestion would be that in this connection the amount of pain or distress inflicted is a side issue. There are perfectly ethical therapeutic or disciplinary procedures, or even games of sport, in which more pain may be suffered than in brainwashing. Brainwashing is unethical basically because it is the ultimate in one-way relationships, where the manipulator not only holds himself invulnerable to the address of his victim, but forcibly re-programmes him so that he becomes in a significant sense a different person, with a *discontinuity* between the new and the old (see next Chapter). In its most extreme imaginable form, this could amount effectively to terminating the psychological life of the former individual and bringing into being (in a second-hand brain and body) somebody new who could not morally be held accountable (or creditable) for any actions taken before the change. We are naturally at a loss for a thought-model in terms of which to deal with such an extreme possibility. If it were ever realized, perhaps for ethical and theological purposes it might most appropriately be thought of by analogy with murder.

Behaviour Control

I have said nothing so far about the more exotic forms of behaviour control beloved of the Sunday supplements – control by means of drugs, electrodes implanted in the brain, and the like. While these things arc already with us in crude forms, their potentialities appear to have been somewhat over-blown, creating exaggerated hopes of the good they can do in remedying psychiatric disorders and exaggerated fears of the power they might offer to a dictatorial government. Scientists closer to the research behind such claims arc more cautious. The neuroscientist Dr. Elliot Valenstein, for example, in a recent paper,[19] takes to task a number of authors including the social psychologist Dr. Kenneth Clark, who in his presidential address to the American Psychological Association ventured to forecast that

> . . . we might be on the threshold of that type of scientific biochemical intervention which could stabilize and make dominant the moral and ethical propensities of man and subordinate, if not eliminate, his negative and primitive behavioral tendencies.

and suggested that political leaders should

> . . . accept and use the earliest perfected form of psychotechnological biochemical interventions which would assure their positive use of power and reduce or block the possibility of using power destructively.

Dr. Valenstein throws cold water on a variety of statements in this vein by different writers, some much less guarded than Dr. Clark.

> 'Even people who should know better,' he says, 'commonly assume that it is possible to arouse distinct motivational states by stimulating specific areas of the brain. It is said that because there are demonstrations of animals made hungry, thirsty, maternal, sexy, and so on, by brain stimulation it is therefore possible to turn such appetites on and off with a great amount of reliability and selectivity. Let me try to

introduce some doubt in your mind about this beautiful story. In my laboratory, we have shown in many different ways that brain stimulation does not duplicate natural motivational states . . . The impression that brain stimulation can evoke the identical emotional state repeatedly in humans is simply a myth perpetuated because of its dramatic impact. *The belief that we can stimulate or destroy a given region of the brain and reliably produce only one type of behavior is sheer fantasy.'*

Without presuming to judge in these controversial matters, it seems fair to conclude that if a dictatorial government wanted to control its population, it would be likely to find some of the older-fashioned methods more cost-effective than either mass brain-implantation or drug-administration; and that the ethical issues raised by these possibilities, though horrifying enough, are not essentially new in principle. It was not yesterday, after all, that Lot's daughters demonstrated the disastrous temporary effects of a drug on their father's priority scheme.[20]

For the present at least manipulation by methods such as Skinnerian reinforcement, which leave the brain uninvaded by either drugs or electrodes, needs closer watching as a realistic hazard.

Conclusion

To sum up, there are clearly grave risks in any mechanistic approach, however well-intentioned, to the shaping of the future of human beings. But I suggest that the obligation to do such good as we can with advancing knowledge cannot be shrugged off by pointing to these risks, or to the low ethical standards and naivety of some of the advocates of human engineering. There are many indications that good can and ought to be done in due course along these lines for our descendants.

While guarding against uncritical enthusiasm, then, it is important to resist the opposite temptation to jump on the scaremongers' bandwagon. Scaremongering sells well in these days of sensation-hungry mass media; but where it distorts and obscures the truth it offends against the human dignity it purports to serve.

The Christian should perhaps be warned in particular against confusing the planned improvement of human health, whether physical, mental or social, with what the New Testament writers mean by 'salvation'. We need only remind ourselves that according to Jesus Christ the healthy are just as much in need of salvation – rescue from rebellious self-sufficiency – as the sick, and may even be harder to bring to recognize their need. There is nothing of 'playing God', nothing either of competing with God or of fighting against God, in trying humanely to apply the gifts of scientific knowledge in this area, any more than in agriculture or medicine.

Finally, it is clear that in face of all this new knowledge the greatest human need is not to learn how to get what we want, but rather to learn what we ought to want. What would count as 'improvement'? What are people for? What is human life for? Confronted with the expanding maze of possible pathways for the human future, people of all religious convictions and of none are nowadays eager to debate such questions. Without pretending to any monopoly of wisdom, Christians should recognize a special obligation to play their part in this collective enterprise, to which the biblical revelation claims such central relevance.

And in case the weight of all this seems too great for the human spirit to bear, there is perhaps some (though not too much) comfort in the thought expressed by Dr. Perry London at the same Wheaton Conference:[14] 'Only the responsibility for the future of man rests with man – not the future of man.'

CHAPTER 5

Mechanism and Meaning

One of the commonest indictments of mechanistic science, in our day especially, is that it 'takes all the meaning out of human life'. I have tried in earlier chapters to show the logical fallacy in this view. We have seen that there is in fact no necessary conflict between mechanistic analysis, even of the human organism itself, and respect for the personal significance and dignity of each human being. So far you might regard this conclusion as rather negative and almost defensive, but in this chapter I want to go a step further, to explore some more positive connections between the mechanistic and the personal levels of understanding man.

Human Communication

As our 'worked example' we shall take the science of human communication.[21] The dignity of man is closely bound up with his powers to communicate. To what extent, then, can we tie together and relate the mechanistic and the meaningful aspects of the process by which human beings communicate with one another? My general theme (as by now you may guess) will be that to take proper account of the mechanistic aspects, far from debunking the meaning of communication, will only sharpen our appreciation of the marvellous process that human communication in fact is.

From an engineering standpoint, supposing we had the privilege of inspecting the inner workings of human beings while they are engaged in communication, what would we expect to see? What are we doing to one another when we communicate with one another? Let us take an example.

Suppose that during a power cut you ask me where the matches are and I say, 'They are on the shelf to your left.' When you hear my reply, you know or believe something that you did not know before; but you may not decide to do anything about it. Indeed, your behaviour may show no external signs of any change resulting from what I have communicated to you. So if we are going to look at the engineering or mechanical level to examine what it is that I am doing to you, it would be no good just studying your behaviour. Assuming that you have heard and understood what I have said, I will have made some changes in you; but the most important ones will doubtless be down at the detailed level of the connections between the nerve cells inside your brain. We do not of course know in detail what the story is there; but again imagining ourselves privileged to study at will different parts of people's brains, it is certainly conceivable that at this engineering level we could identify the changes that occur when I tell you that the matches are on the shelf to your left.

This leads us to ask what kind of change – which changes at the mechanistic level – I am *trying* to bring about. What I am doing in physical terms is to wobble some parts of my face up and down and expel pulses of air through them, so that sound waves impinge on your auditory meatus and eventually cause electrical impulses to travel up your auditory nerve. Thereafter we get lost in a complicated physico-chemical story about the depths of your nervous system. Even if we knew all the details, I suspect that at this level we would get so bogged down that we would miss the point.

Fortunately for our purpose there is an intermediate level at which we can talk about it more concisely – the level of communication engineering, at which we concentrate on the *repertoire* of different ways of acting in the world, from which the brain has to make a running selection. At this level we are not going to talk about you as a mass of nerve cells and chemicals interacting, but rather as an organism with a certain range of skills in moving about in the world and bringing about changes in the world. When I tell you that the match box is to your left, I am not necessarily trying to make you reach out for it. What I am trying to do is rather to shape what we might call your *conditional readiness to reckon with* the match box: I want you to be ready to look for it there *if* circumstances arose when you needed it. This is a typical example of communication, where I am trying to transfer to you not a *thing* but a *form*, a state of organization. If I know where the matches are, my brain is conditionally organized so that if and when I want them I am ready to act appropriately. By speaking to you I am trying to set you up so that you are similarly 'conditionally ready' to find them. At this level, then, we have identified physical happenings in the mechanism of your brain which in a clear sense betoken the *meaning* of what you took me to be saying.

Perhaps a simple analogy may help.[22] In a railway shunting yard you will find a signal box full of levers. When the levers are set up in a certain pattern, there may in fact be nothing happening in the shunting yard at the time; but according to the way the signals are set up, the yard is 'conditionally ready' to deal with traffic in a corresponding way. If you change the switches, its conditional readiness to cope with the traffic will change, even though no traffic may be passing at the time. This is of course only a very crude image of what goes on inside our heads when we communicate with one another; but it will serve to illustrate the function of communication. We can think of words as specially designed tools, or component parts of tools, for adjusting the 'switch-settings' of the brain. Uttering a message is rather like reaching out with a tool, not necessarily to make one another do things, but to change the signal levers, metaphorically speaking, in one another's organizing mechanism so that we become *conditionally* ready to act differently.

In terms of this kind of image, then, it is not too difficult to see a link between what might at first sight seem completely unrelated, namely the mechanical aspects of a communication and its meaning. When I tell you that the matches are on the shelf, and you believe me, the meaning of that belief will be represented in your brain by corresponding *constraints* (and enablements) on your repertoire of readinesses for action. Your brain will now have 'switch settings' which in given circumstances will shape your behaviour in an appropriate way, whereas with a different belief – with different switch settings – your behaviour would have been shaped differently in the same circumstances. I am not of course implying that beliefs or meanings *are* states of the brain; that would be a linguistic blunder. I mean that they are *represented* by such states, in the sense in which a message chalked on a blackboard is represented by the distribution of chalk. My point is that in these mechanistic terms we can find ready *correlates* for such concepts as meaning and belief.

Failure of Communication

Communication, alas, is not always successful. In general, the change that takes place in your conditional readiness in response to my message may not be exactly the change I intend. We need to distinguish carefully between the *intended* meaning and the *received* meaning of my communication. The intended meaning is represented by the shaping adjustment that I was trying to bring about; the received meaning, the meaning that you take, is represented by the adjustment that actually comes about in your organizing mechanism.

Another analogy may help us to understand the different kinds of obstacles that may prevent communication from being accurate or meaningful. The ignition key of your car, at the physical level, is a piece of metal with notches cut in it. If someone asks you why you value the key, you would answer not in terms of the metal of which it is made, but in terms of its power to switch on your car engine. The key has a certain 'opening power' in relation to the lock on the ignition switch. Relative to the lock on someone else's car, its opening power would presumably be nil; though there may well be other locks on your own car for which its opening power is one hundred per cent.

I find it helpful to think of the meaning of a message as something rather like the opening power of a key. A message is a tool for setting up a particular state of readiness in the receiver; a key is a tool for setting up another kind of readiness in a lock, namely readiness to open if turned. If the key is the wrong shape, then either it will not fit into the lock at all, or it will not line up the wards correctly so that the lock can open, so it will have no opening power relative to that lock. The opening power of the key, then, is a *relation* which depends both on the shape of the key and on the structure of the lock. Deficiencies in either (or both) can cause failure to open.

In just the same way, I am suggesting that we think of the meaning of a communication as a *relation*, between the shape of the communication signal on the one hand, and the structure of the organizing mechanism in the brain of the person receiving the communication on the other. The same signal may have two different meanings for two receivers, and be meaningless for a third; and none of them may get the meaning intended by the originator. Unless their organizing system has the kind of repertoire envisaged by the originator, some failure of communication is inevitable.

I have thought it worthwhile to spell this out for two reasons. In the first place, it illustrates yet again the constructive harmony that exists between the levels of mechanism and of meaning. There is obviously here no question of pitting one against the other. But secondly, I think that the mechanistic level of analysis can help us to ward off any idea that because meaning is relative, questions of meaning are in the last analysis 'purely subjective' and arbitrary. From the engineering standpoint, nothing could be further from the truth. The fact that a given message means different things to two different individuals does not in the least imply that either of them is entitled to take from it any meaning he likes. At the mechanical level, the meaning for each of them will be a perfectly definite relation, which a super-scientist who knew enough about his brain could in principle establish objectively: just as objectively as a locksmith could establish the opening power of a particular key for a particular lock, without even trying it, from a knowledge of their respective structures. I emphasize this point because there are those who like to use 'relativity' as an excuse for dismissing the idea of absolute truth, and paying no attention to absolute claims, on the grounds that 'everything is relative'. There is no suggestion of support for this kind of talk from the engineering level, and an information engineer would have no patience with it. However difficult it might be to establish the relevant data in practice, he would insist that in principle both the intended meaning and the received meaning of a communication for any recipient are matters of objective fact. Thus an engineering analysis of the process of communication, so far from debunking its meaningfulness, only helps to sharpen up the precision with which we understand what is going on when people communicate.

Conceptual Blind Spots

What more can we say at the mechanistic level about the conditions that must be met if communication is to be meaningful? Take again the example of the matchbox. Before you can understand my saying that it lies to your left, there must be some kind of possible action or planning of action on your part to which this information would be relevant. Again, to understand my calling it a matchbox, you must have other relevant ingredients in your total repertoire, internal or external. The general point is that unless your total repertoire includes the appropriate capacities for action, internal or external, a message which is designed to shape your conditional readiness for such action can have no 'shaping power' for you – it will be meaningless for you.

Once again this would be an immensely complex criterion to apply in practice; but my point is that it shows the question of meaningfulness to be a strictly objective one. It also makes clear at this level why the understanding of a sentence requires much more than the ability to follow logical rules in manipulating symbols. Understanding requires that you have the internal repertoire to which the message is addressed. Without those ingredients you may be completely precluded from grasping the point being made: you will suffer from *conceptual blind spots,* because you have nothing in your organizing mechanism to be shaped in the way intended.

By the same token, when you *believe* something, this implies that you have accepted corresponding constraints on your planning of relevant action. What you believe is something you 'reckon with' or 'take into account' in any relevant planning. At the mechanistic level, this implies that an imaginary superscientist who could examine all your brain's 'switch-settings' would be able to read off what you really believe (as distinct from the formulae you would be prepared to repeat) in terms of the corresponding constraints he could identify in your organizing repertoire. (It would, I think, do none of us any harm to test what we call our religious beliefs by this mechanistic criterion: What story would a perfectly-informed brain-engineer be able to tell about our internal readinesses for action and the planning of action?)

We can take this mechanistic line a step further. Not only believing a communication, but even *imagining* a state of affairs, will have its necessary mechanical correlates. If I invite you to imagine, say, a nice juicy steak, then at the mechanistic level I am trying to set running in your organizing system some of the processes that would be set running if you saw a steak. You might salivate, for example, or wince if you happen to be a vegetarian. In any case, you would be *physically changed* as a result of my invitation. Mechanisms would be running or ready to run in your brain that would otherwise have been in a different state.

The point I am making is that nothing at the conceptual level, no communication of any kind, can claim to be *neutral.* Some internal machinery must be devoted to representing anything that is perceived or thought about or talked about. Thinking is not neutral; looking or listening are not neutral;

imagining is not neutral; even asking a question is not neutral at the mechanical level. After any such conceptual activity your physical organizing system, as an engineer would see it, has been set running in a new pattern; in some respect your conditional readiness is different, for good or ill, from now on.

Vulnerability

Thus from the standpoint of mechanistic brain science the old-fashioned 'liberal' idea that it can never do harm to listen to any argument and 'follow it wherever it may lead' appears dangerously naive and highly implausible. All our evidence suggests that in human communication, mechanism and meaning are so inextricably interwoven that by communicating with a man you cannot avoid effecting physical changes in him, some of which may not be reversible, just as surely and as fatefully as if you laid forceful hands on him; and this is true even if you only ask him a question. 'Yea, hath God said . . . ?' (*Genesis* 3:1). So this engineering level of analysis really rubs in on us our vulnerability in face of one another's communications, and the responsibility that we have for the causal implications of what we say to one another. In our society the power of others to make physical changes in our brains by *direct* physical assault is reasonably limited both by law and by the thickness of our skulls; but at the 'informational' or 'programming' level it is astonishingly unrestricted. We have only to think how jealously a computer operator would guard his programmes from unwarranted interference to realize just how surprising this is. Part of the explanation may lie in a hangover of the old-fashioned materialistic notion that only physical damage is 'real' damage. Information, however polluting to the spirit, is thought of as 'all in the mind' and so somehow 'unreal'. Even if the materialistic criterion were accepted, however, mechanistic brain science would have none of this nonsense. Information has effects – for good or ill – which are just as material as those of ale or arsenic or the virus of polio. Conceptual pollution is a reality at least as objectively identifiable in principle as environmental pollution, in terms of its damaging effect on the conditional readiness of those who suffer from it.

I stress this because the suggestion is sometimes put about that only the unduly 'tender-minded' worry about such things as cultural pollution; for the sufficiently 'tough-minded' the problem is supposed to be non-existent. The truth, I suggest, is the reverse. It is from the most tough-minded scientific standpoint that we can most clearly see through the protestations of those who pollute our media of communication in the name of 'freedom of speech'. Here particularly the human sciences have a constructive part to play in fostering the dignity of man.

The need for an initiative in this direction is becoming recognized even at the international level. As a leading article in *The Times* put it, when commenting on a Unesco Conference in 1970, 'The creation of a healthy culture, that is an aesthetic and intellectual environment favourable to the psychological growth of the individual in society, is not a matter inside the competence of international bodies, however well-meaning. International bodies and national governments can however act either to encourage or to remove the pollutions of culture, those influences which have a deforming or limiting effect on human life. Those pollutions are of as many kinds as the pollutions of the physical environment.' As examples the writer takes the growth of pornography ('not an affirmation but a denial of life') and 'the hostility to meaning of some of the artists of the 1960s'. 'We need to return to a higher sense of responsibility for and in the broadcasting media and in the press as well,' he says. 'We need to oppose the anti-cultures of our age. The counter-attack on the pollution of our physical environment has, thank goodness, begun; the counter-attack on the even more serious pollution of our cultural environment needs to be started.'[23]

To follow up this topic adequately would take us too far from our present subject; but from our present scientific perspective it seems clear that realistic compassion and respect for human dignity require a concern for conceptual hygiene no less stringent than our accepted concern for physical hygiene. Minimal sanitary precautions can be irksome and are indeed costly, but we have agreed (or at least are requested) to observe them out of respect and concern for the health and dignity of our community. No claptrap about 'infringements of liberty' would persuade us to return to the plague-ridden medieval conditions from which these precautions have released us. How many generations must pass, I wonder, before our present lack of precautions against conceptual and cultural pollution will seem equally uncivilized?

Of course, we have only to look at the growth of self-propagating bureaucracy in our day to realize that human dignity can be equally endangered by excessive restrictions on freedom to communicate. The abominable affronts to the free spirit suffered today by some Christians and Jews in the U.S.S.R. are a vivid warning of the need to keep central regulation to an absolute minimum. In the field of medical hygiene (except during epidemics) this can safely be done, thanks to the internal defence force of antibodies that we all acquire naturally. In the case of conceptual hygiene, it would be nice to think that a healthy society would similarly pass on to each generation enough spiritual 'antibodies' to make them immune against any infections sprayed on them by diseased users of communication media. Doubtless this is what Paul had in mind in offering his famous admonition:[24] 'Whatsoever things are lovely, . . . pure, . . . and of good report, think on these things.' Certainly it is arguable that the more our mass media did to disseminate positively health-giving ideas, the less stringent could be the restrictions that would suffice against the spread of diseases of the spirit. A splendid lead in this direction was offered in a recent article in *The Times*[25] by Dr. J. H. Court, Senior Lecturer in Psychology at Flinders University, South Australia. Instead of thinking negatively in terms of 'censorship', he suggests that the issue be considered as one of *quality control*. 'Every production-line worker and every ecologist knows that quality can be maintained only by a ruthless approach to the sub-standard product or the noxious pollutant. In the realm of art and literature it could be worth asking "Is it good enough to be acceptable?" rather than "Is it bad enough to ban?" . . . Some will argue that there is no basis for standards whereby quality control can be established. With that fundamentally amoral stance there is no basis for discussion. There is, however, the evidence of our time that the primitive, the debased and the obscene is elevated to the status of art when the pursuit of good is rejected. The sad obverse of this is that a corresponding decline occurs in the production of those fine arts which have been among the ennobling aspects of our civilization. The implementation of effective quality control of literature and films will undoubtedly be in the public good.'

Some people may be inclined to feel that provided what is communicated is true there should be no restriction on its propagation. If 'the truth shall make you free' (John 8:32), they might argue, surely we can never have too much of it? But this is not good enough. In the first place, it tears the original from its context. What Jesus actually says is: *'If you continue in my word . . . you shall know the truth, and the truth shall make you free.'* There is no suggestion that all true information is *ipso facto* liberating. Indeed it is easy to think of obvious counter-examples. To hold up a mirror to a tight-rope walker, for example, might be quite the reverse! To tell all your friends everything that you think about them, or hear said about them, might drive them neurotic rather than set them free. To 'hold up a mirror to society' is equally manipulative, and no more guaranteed to be beneficial. *Freedom not to know* is at least as clearly defensible a human right as freedom of speech. Perhaps it has been unduly neglected.

Positivism

Mechanistic analysis can also help us to see how superficial is the 'logical positivist' rejection of religious language as 'meaningless'.[26] This argument, or dogma rather, used to have quite a vogue among unbelievers. The claim was that a statement could not be accepted as meaningful unless you could specify at least in principle how it could be verified or falsified. Now in science this is quite a good discipline. If somebody claims that he has a certain kind of particle in a box, then it is perfectly fair to ask him what kind of public observation (at least in principle) would test his statement. If no answer can be given, a scientist feels justified in dismissing the claim as 'scientifically meaningless'. The trouble is that this principle was transferred by some philosophers, particularly those with anti-religious axes to grind, to domains of human discourse where it makes no sense.

Some Christians have tried to meet such attacks by citing special cases of religious statements – about the end of the world, for example – where in principle verification would one day be possible. This is all very well as far as it goes; but it is surely the case that much of the discourse of biblical religion is about God, who is not accessible to observation, or else about human experiences that are private and do not necessarily show themselves immediately in observable behaviour. For example, if a man says 'God has forgiven me', it is not obvious how his claim could ever be publicly tested.

Must we then dismiss all such claims as meaningless? I do not think so. Once again, our mechanistic approach suggests a criterion that is much less arbitrary and question-begging. Suppose we had the privilege of inspecting the organizing machinery of a man engaged in religious conversation. The basic question that a mechanistic scientist would ask in order to check the meaningfulness of what is being said is: *What shaping job* is this statement designed to do? We find in the Bible, for example, the statement that God is willing to forgive the penitent sinner, indeed more willing than the penitent sinner is to ask forgiveness. What shaping job is this designed to do? Does it have a shaping function for the listener? Here we return to the various points made earlier. First, the statement may exercise little or no shaping function on anyone who is deficient in the internal repertoire on which it is designed to do its work. For example, anyone who finds himself unable to repent, or refuses to recognize responsibility, may be expected to find no meaning in talk about God's forgiveness, because the appropriate repertoire is not there to be shaped. Again, anyone who uses religious terms habitually for other purposes, so that he finds himself shaped into quite different conditional readinesses from those intended, may judge such statements if not meaningless then certainly bizarre by comparison with their intended meaning.

The point I am making is that by carrying our questions of meaningfulness down to the engineering level, we can in principle distinguish between meaningful and meaningless communication even in situations where there is no question whatever of verification by public procedures. We can also distinguish two different kinds of failure of communication, relevant in particular to the domain of religious discourse: One, where people actually lack, for whatever reason, some of the conditional readinesses upon which the communication is designed to work; and the other, where different components of the message select component readinesses which are incompatible. This is of course particularly common where religious language uses metaphor.

The classic statement in the New Testament about conceptual blind spots, where people miss the point even though appropriate words are being used correctly, is Paul's in I Corinthians 2:14 – 'The natural man receives not the things of the spirit of God, for they are foolishness to him.' In our terms, this implies that it is possible for a man, though psychologically perfectly normal, to be yet so lacking in his repertoire of readinesses (the things that he is prepared to contemplate doing) that some biblical doctrines will be meaningless to him. They will have no shaping function on his states of readiness; they will not be able to exercise the shaping function that they are intended to carry out, even in his imagination.

We will return in the last chapter to the question how such a condition can be remedied – how conceptual blind spots can be removed. Meantime, let me make just one further point. Once we take seriously the way in which a message depends for its meaningfulness on the repertoire of the receiver, this removes the sting from a great deal of psychological speculation as to how religious concepts arise. For example, Sigmund Freud made a lot of anti-religious play with the idea that God was a 'father figure' – that the idea of God was simply some kind of transformation of the idea of a father, and therefore (by Freudian logic) 'illusory'. But of course this begs the whole question. For just suppose (to put it neutrally) that there is God; just suppose that we owe our being to a Creator who wants to make himself known to us, to communicate with us. This means that at the mechanical level he will want us somehow to develop the appropriate internal apparatus upon which his communications can have their shaping functions. We must, in other words, undergo a chain of experience through which our brains develop internal symbols that correspond adequately to what he wants to talk to us about. And if in our world he has designed the family, with its father–son relationship, as the natural environment in which these internal symbols can develop, this does nothing logically to debunk or make meaningless or false what he then proceeds to say to us, any more than an understanding of the brain processes that develop our ability to recognize words debunks the meaning of what we then read. The whole question of the origin-in-time of our religious concepts at the psychological level is neutral *vis-à-vis* the truth of what is then said in the religious terms. Once you take seriously the mechanistic requirements for meaningful communication, there is in principle no threat in speculations by Freud and others as to the importance of our infant experience of 'father figures' and the like for our understanding of religious discourse. It is exactly what we should expect if we have a Creator who wants us to understand in some dim way what he reveals of himself and his purposes. If Freud's particular speculations turn out to be wrong, then I as a Christian see no reason to doubt that some other story at the same general mechanistic level ought to be true.

Integrity in Communication

It will be obvious from what I have said already that the mechanistic analysis of communication offers in principle a much sharper criterion of truthfulness and integrity than conventional logical analysis of the propositions in which information is expressed. If we imagine an engineer able to monitor the brain of the sender of a message, and also the effects produced in the brain of the recipient, it is clear that 'truthfulness' for him would be judged not at the superficial level of the words used but much more stringently in terms of the total *shaping operations* intended and achieved. For him the shaping effects of context, intonation and similar 'intangibles' would be as obvious and significant as those of printed words. He would see it as a mere historical accident that we happen to have no written symbols for the 'non-verbal' components of such operations, and would be correspondingly equipped to identify forms of inconsistency and deception that might pass easily through the logician's net. Think for example of the famous occasion on which (it is said) an Archbishop arriving in New York was asked by reporters whether he would be visiting any nightclubs. Being English, the visitor raised an eyebrow and asked, '*are* there any nightclubs in New York?' He was duly reported in jubilant headlines: 'Archbishop's first question on reaching New York: Are there any nightclubs?' It is when we analyze the total shaping function of such a statement with the eye of an engineer that its untruthfulness is manifest. A traditional logician would have to pass it as simply 'true'.

There is, I think, a particular moral here for religious communication. From an engineering standpoint it would be quite artificial to separate verbal from non-verbal aspects of praying, preaching or praising. All contribute to the total communicative function, just as all the ridges on a car key contribute to its opening power.[27] Inconsistency between verbal and non-verbal aspects can be fully as disastrous to total function as purely verbal contradiction. The man who purports to lead prayers to God in a tone that means 'Here's what it says in the book', or 'Now then, folks, what do you say in response?', is emitting a self-contradictory nonsense. A preacher who talks about God as if he had forgotten that he was in God's very presence may say nothing theologically false, and yet destroy the whole communicative fabric of his sermon.

The same risk of self-contradiction attends the present fashion of setting sacred words to ha-cha-cha rhythms. I think we need sometimes to be more *biologically* sensitive to what these rhythms do to us – the kind of shaping functions they exercise in their own right on our conditional readinesses. We might then consider in all seriousness whether some of the non-verbal signals so conveyed may not effectively contradict or make nonsense of the verbal component. It might do us no harm to be asked by a sceptical listener: If you really meant even one-tenth of what you are saying or singing, could you possibly say it or sing it *like that*? Do you realize *what else* you are saying in the non-verbal code you are using? It would be no answer to protest that such rhythms are found natural and appropriate by tribal Africans who become Christian. What the sceptic said was: 'If *you* really meant one-tenth of what *you* are saying . . .' If you do not happen to be a tribal African, you cannot dodge the issue by imagining that you are. The objective question is what shaping function these things have for *you*, and those with whom you share them. What associations do they have? Which of your readinesses do they enhance, and which do they inhibit? It is precisely because these matters are relative that we must take pains to be objective about them in each individual case. Here as elsewhere, a proper recognition of relativity does not mean that 'anything goes': it means that more effort, rather than less, will be needed in order to discriminate realistically between what does and what does not 'go'.

In case anyone is tempted to dismiss all this as a 'rationalization of conservative prejudice' (one of Screwtape's favourite fog-making phrases), it may be worth pointing out that the sceptic could ask the same question about a lot of conventional hymn singing, bible reading and the like. My point is not that an engineering perspective favours one tradition over against another, but rather that it helps to bring some objectivity into an area where issues are too often debated in terms of subjective preference and prejudice, by introducing more deep-going criteria of integrity. So far from debunking the significance of worship as dialogue with our all-holy Creator, it offers positive help in remembering that 'all things are naked and opened unto the eyes of Him with whom we have to do'. (Hebrews 4:13 AV)

Brainwashing and Conversion

Having looked at the mechanistic aspects of communication in general, it is perhaps time to return to the question of evangelism and its relation to brainwashing, which we touched upon in the last chapter. Evangelistic preaching, like any other form of communication, is of course intended to mould and shape the conditional readinesses of the hearers; but there is a world of difference between honest straightforward evangelism and the kind of calculated manipulation that constitutes brainwashing. What is objectionable in brainwashing, whether religious or otherwise, is not that it stirs the emotions, or employs dramatic imagery and the like, but that it does these things in such a way as to *stifle* men's rational faculties instead of enlightening them. There is nothing intrinsically wrong in using rhetorical skills to open people's eyes to the truth and to urge them to forsake all else to follow its implications. But the brainwasher plies his art in such a way as to deflect attention *away* from inconvenient things known or believed to be true by his victims, in order to gain acceptance for things he cannot adequately substantiate. In the limit, as mentioned in Chapter 4, he can cause such discontinuities in the organization of the brain as to destroy the identity of the individual. The end-product of his activities is in an important sense *not the same individual* as the one who came in for his treatment.

To see what this means, think of the kind of chess problem that you find on the back pages of newspapers. White has to checkmate with his Queen in three moves, let us say. To someone who cared nothing for the rules of chess there might seem to be a simple solution – just lift the Queen from wherever she happens to be, and put her down where the King cannot escape her. The objection to this, of course, is not only that it cheats, but that it makes the final phase the ending of *a different game* from the one we were invited to finish. In chess terms, there would be a discontinuity between the situations before and after the rules were violated.

By the same token, if by brainwashing techniques the principles of organization of a man's personality were so overwhelmed as to bring about an essential discontinuity in his mental history (analogous to that which rule-breaking brings about in the history of a chess-game), then the original individual has not only had unethical violence done to him; in an important sense he has been destroyed, and a new individual now lives in his body.

But, someone may say, is not this just the kind of language used in the Bible to describe religious conversion? Do Christians not have to 'die to sin'? Has not Paul said,[28] 'I live – yet not I, but Christ lives in me'? Why then should not an evangelist use brainwashing techniques to bring about such a radical change? The biblical answer, of course, is that the discontinuity in Christian conversion is not one of personal *identity* but of personal *priorities*. When our eyes have been opened by the Spirit of God to see the awful truth about our situation as rebels against our Creator, and the shamefulness of our poisoned priority scheme, we may well experience an emetic spiritual reaction that leaves us purged of many of our former characteristics; but our minds in all this are meant to be fully alert and active and unviolated. There is complete continuity of personality between the man whom Christ implores[29] to 'be reconciled to God' and the same man rescued and 're-born to newness of life'. However deep the emotional experience of reconciliation, there is no biblical substitute for the intelligent personal acknowledgement of, and response to, the realities of the situation. Any method of evangelism that seeks violently to bypass or override the intellectual faculties can at most produce a spiritual monstrosity – someone whose mental history is discontinuous from that of the individual he once was, so that the problem of his guilty past has never been resolved, and his 'conversion' can only be correspondingly shallow.

None of this denies for a moment that psychological knowledge may be helpful (as other sciences are) in alleviating the *symptoms* of our broken relationship with God, including our tendencies to anti-social actions and attitudes. But the *cure* – the forgiveness of God – can be received only at the personal level by a man in full possession of all his faculties. There is no substitute for personal reconciliation in mechanical manipulation. The mass evangelist ought to know about brainwashing techniques for the same reason that a dietician ought to know about poisons – not in order to use them, but in order to avoid damaging those towards whom he has responsibility.

Beginnings and Endings

The argument throughout these lectures has been that we can harmoniously integrate the physical and the personal aspects of human nature if we regard each conscious individual as embodied in his cerebral process, in something of the sense in which a message is embodied in a communication signal. In this sense my activity – the activity I am aware of from my standpoint as a conscious agent – is the *meaning* of the bodily activity you recognize as mine. The total activity of my body (especially of my central nervous system) *betokens* my conscious thinking, doing and suffering – which, you remember, are facts of experience I would be lying to deny. But if we were to agree on this as a working postulate you might still feel inclined to press two final questions: how does a human organism come to acquire its personal meaning? And what happens to this when the body is destroyed at death? Can such a view of the unity of man fit in with the Christian doctrine of our eternal destiny?

In relation to each of these questions we must be on our guard against the mistaken form of reasoning to which I referred in Chapter 3 as 'thin-end-of-the-wedgery'. A thin-end-of-the-wedger would argue that if you cannot decide exactly how many hairs make a beard, you will have to conclude that there is no 'real' difference between being bearded and being clean-shaven. If you denied that a man with only one hair on his chin was bearded, that would be the 'thin end of the wedge' which could drive you into admitting that no chin, however many hairs it sprouted, 'really' had a beard.

The parallel to this silly doctrine in relation to human consciousness goes by the name of 'panpsychism'. Popularized recently by such writers as Teilhard de Chardin, it has an ancient history. Put crudely, the argument is that if a full-grown human body has a conscious 'inner aspect', then all the matter of which it is composed must have some degree of consciousness. Logically, this is rather like arguing that if a triangle is composed of three lines, there must be some degree of triangularity in each of the lines! The theory also has to import special assumptions to account for the fact that a man can lose consciousness or fall asleep while his body still contains the same total of physical matter, organized in a structure with the same degree of complexity, as when he is conscious. For these and other reasons I feel there is little in favour of the view that we acquire consciousness as infants simply by accumulating enough matter in a sufficiently complex structure. On the other hand I can see equally little reason to think of consciousness as a kind of invisible stuff which floats into the body at a particular stage in early life.

An alternative that I believe fits with all the data is to think of 'becoming conscious' in the way we think of 'catching fire'.

Consciousness would then be something we would in principle recognize by the particular dance of brain activity that expresses it, just as a fire is recognized by the dance of its flames. As such it is no doubt a condition shared with many lower animals. What distinguishes human consciousness (as far as we know) is its peculiar *self-reflecting* character – the fact that thanks to our internal communicative apparatus we can represent ourselves, as well as other people, articulately to ourselves. This articulate personal self-awareness is something that presumably develops in early infancy through our normal interactions with parents and others. In these terms it is not so much something we have in *addition* to our conscious experience, as a specific *quality* that distinguishes human conscious experience. It originates, as far as we know, in the experience of being *treated-as-a-person* by those who are already persons. The question when a human organism becomes a *person* is thus logically distinct from the question when it becomes *conscious*. From this standpoint the old chestnut: 'At what point does the soul enter the body?' breaks up into a cluster of interrelated questions. One is: 'At what point does the bodily activity signify conscious agency?' Another is: 'At what point does it acquire *personal* significance of the *self*-conscious kind that we all undeniably experience at first hand?' The process of acquiring significance of either kind could of course be a gradual one with no sharply-defined transition point; or it could be as abrupt and definite as the ignition of an inflammable mixture. This technical question may be resolved as we discover more about what goes on in the brain in sleep and wakefulness, and the physiological basis of unconsciousness. In either case, there would be no need to deny that the transition resulted from a *continuous* quantitative change in the physical factors that made it possible, in order to affirm that the conscious human person is qualitatively different from the unconscious human body.

    In line with this idea, I suggest that we can think of the personal significance of a human being as something normally passed on like a flame from parents to children through the experience of dialogue. By this I mean not simply that we learn from experience to *treat* one another as conscious persons, as if consciousness were a matter of convention, but that it is in this way that we *become* conscious persons as a matter of fact. It may sometimes be necessary, in the clinic for example, to use conventional criteria to decide whether a particular patient is or is not conscious; but the question at issue is always one of fact, on which we may be right or wrong: Is there in front of us an individual who is conscious of our presence (or of pain or distress or whatever) as we undeniably are of his? For the Christian, of course, this will be recognized as a fact known to the Creator, who in the last analysis is the Giver of personal significance to each human being who comes into existence; so that any idea of reducing it to a matter of human convention would be absurd.

What then of the other end of the human time-scale? To ask 'at what point does the soul or the spirit leave the body' is a very natural way of expressing our puzzlement over the phenomenon of death; but in the light of what we have said it may have misleading overtones, suggesting as it does the image of an invisible pilot leaving a cockpit, or an invisible substance escaping from a container. Let us try an alternative: At what point does the bodily activity lose its personal significance? The answer in terms of our technical metaphor would be: when the 'flame' goes out. Once the central nervous system can no longer sustain the flicker of self-reflecting activity that embodies conscious personal experience, its remaining activity, however elaborate and prolonged, is not that of a 'living soul' in the biblical sense, still less that of a 'human spirit'.

Some people cling to the image of an invisible substance leaving the body in the belief that if they give this up they will have abandoned any possibility of 'life after death'. If a flame goes out, they might say, that is surely the end of it for ever. I would certainly agree that at death our physical remains lose their personal significance, and that that is normally the end of our existence in this world of space and time. But to leave the matter there would be to leave out the whole dimension of our relationship with, and dependence on, our extra-temporal Creator. As we shall remind ourselves in the next chapter, the biblical promise is that the relationship with God established during our lifetime, for good or ill, is something eternal, which is only sealed, and not broken, by our death. If it is our Creator's will that we shall again have our being as conscious agents in his presence, the provision of an appropriate body will be up to him. The fate of our present embodiment is of no consequence. The biblical promise is that we shall be 'raised to life' in a fresh embodiment, perhaps radically different from our present one (see I Cor. 15), but still bearing the same personal significance. All this, with the glorious hope held out by Christ's resurrection, is fully as compatible with the view outlined above as with the more traditional imagery.

Conclusion

In any context, whether psychological or moral or spiritual, the idea that mechanistic analysis destroys or damages personal significance is a mistake. Although one particular thought-model of man, as a mechanical body piloted by an immaterial driver, may lead to embarrassments of various kinds, no such embarrassments attend the idea that my conscious agency is the personal significance to be attached (because attached by my Creator) to the activity that is my embodiment, just as a message is the significance to be attached (because attached by its originator) to the physical activity that embodies it. Christians in particular have every incentive to take seriously and thankfully anything we can learn about the mechanistic aspect as something complementary to the personal; for it can only sharpen our appreciation of the responsibility we bear towards one another as vulnerable moral beings with an eternal destiny.

CHAPTER 6

The Truest Dignity

In the last chapter, when we were looking at the mechanics of communication, we saw that what makes a belief meaningful is the constraints that it imposes on what we called the conditional readinesses of the person who entertains the belief. We took the engineer's standpoint and looked at the human organism as a vastly complex repertoire of different components of modes of action, including internal action on its own organizing system. Meaningful communication we saw as communication which was able to shape or mould the recipient's conditional readinesses, for action or the planning of action. If the repertoire was deficient in a particular group of readinesses, then we saw that this would lead to a corresponding conceptual blind spot. Talk in that area of discourse would be *meaningless* to the individual.

Now, according to the Christian religion, man finds his truest dignity in facing up to his obligations towards the God who continually gives him his being. But there are many people in our day who find talk of this kind totally meaningless. They seem, according to themselves, to have a blind spot for talk about God. Is this then something that we can discuss only in theological terms? Is it enough to say simply that 'the god of this world has blinded their minds'; or is there something in our present mechanistic approach which might help us to understand further how blind spots of this sort can arise, and what must happen if they are to be remedied? These are the questions we must now explore.

How Repertoires Develop

The central idea we shall be working out is that conceptual blind spots arise wherever there are corresponding gaps in our repertoire. This leads us to ask first how repertoires develop in general. In the lowliest organisms it is mainly a matter of genetic specification. From what we saw of the genetic machinery in Chapter 4, it is not surprising that the spider's capacity for web spinning, for example, or the bird's for nest building, is not something acquired by imitation of others, but depends mainly on inbuilt genetic instructions. These are examples of what we might call a 'special purpose' repertoire, and the book by W. H. Thorpe to which I referred in Chapter 3 gives many beautiful examples of the prefabricated readinesses for action which the genes can build into such organisms. Usually these are conditional readinesses, waiting to be triggered by particular episodes, or particular features of the environment impinging on the sense organs of the animal, into releasing what might be called 'subroutines': little programmes ready to run off a complex pattern of behaviour as a stereotyped sequence. The baby gosling, for example, comes out of the egg all ready to follow for dear life the first sizeable moving object that fulfils certain preset conditions. Normally, this would be its mother; but as Konrad Lorenz[30] showed, it could be the boots of the scientist who stood around while it was hatching! The newborn lamb finds its mother's undercarriage irresistibly buttable at first sight; and so on.

There is increasing evidence that this is true to some extent not only of lower animals but even of human beings. For instance, the human infant is well programmed at birth to know what to do with a nipple. It has also been found that very young babies smile in a more or less automatic fashion to face-like cartoons, and they have many other inbuilt component subroutines for sexual and social perception and behaviour. According to the linguist, Noam Chomsky, human beings even have some genetically inbuilt conditional readinesses for language. Since in lower animals these readinesses can be so amazingly specific, I would suggest that Christians certainly need not be surprised if in due course we find a genetic basis even for certain basic aspects of human moral and religious perception and behaviour. This, after all, would be only the counterpart at the scientific level of the ancient affirmation of St. Augustine: 'Thou hast made us for thyself, and our hearts are restless until they find rest in Thee.' If it is true that God has made us for himself, then it would hardly be surprising to find something to correspond to this in the genetic instructions that determine the make-up of a man. Without God man is essentially incomplete, starved of something for which his genetic equipment prepares him.

But genetics of course is only part of this story. The last ten or twenty years have brought a flood of fresh evidence on the essential part played by early experience in *exercising* the special-purpose computing mechanisms that respond to various trigger features. For example, although nerve cells in the visual system of mammals come ready-made to respond to lines or edges at particular orientations, nevertheless if the animal's eyes are covered with a diffusing screen from birth these cells lose their sensitivity. This principle seems to apply quite generally. In-built facilities, if they are not exercised, tend to atrophy; so experience, as well as genetic instruction, is essential in that sense to the normal development of the repertoire.

The higher we go in the animal kingdom, the more general-purpose the equipment becomes. Whereas spiders, for example, are almost entirely controlled by special-purpose pre-programmed units, in the higher animals there is more and more flexibility. To give you just one example, in the eye of a frog there are nerve cells linked with others so as to form micro-computers which are triggered by objects the size of a fly moving over a leaf-like background, or objects moving in a particular direction. In the monkey's eye, however, the nerve cells are more general-purpose; they do not have these special connections to make them sensitive to such specific features. Instead, this function is transferred to a higher level of the monkey's nervous system.

Now the human central nervous system has by far the greatest proportion of what the anatomists call 'uncommitted cortex': regions not pre-committed by construction to one special-purpose job. Our brains have the greatest plasticity, the greatest openness to be moulded by experience, of all the animal kingdom. As we have seen, we profit from this by communicating with one another in particularly elaborate and subtle ways, shaping and enlarging one another's internal repertoires by long and complex processes which include what we call training and education. The proper balancing of this early diet of experience, for example in the relation of parents to children, has also much to do with the development of normal healthy moral and religious awareness.

Since the human brain is so plastic, so richly endowed with general-purpose components, you might imagine that all conceptual blind spots could in principle be remedied simply by telling the individual what he needs to know. There is, however, a further technical complication to be reckoned with, which arises from the possibility of *self-adjustment*. With such an elaborate and powerful repertoire of skills for adjusting readinesses and priorities in other people, there goes a correspondingly complex power to turn this equipment inward upon the system itself, so that the individual to some extent assumes *control of his own priorities*. According to current theory of brain function, this indeed may be the mechanistic correlate of what we call *deliberating*. Deliberating, like thinking in general, is likely to involve much of the machinery that is used when we talk to somebody else, only it runs in an 'inwardly directed' mode so that our organizing system is now adjusting its own readinesses and priorities rather than somebody else's.

The Perils of Self-adjustment

You can see that there is a risk here. A system that gets hold of its own controls can easily run amok. To get some feeling for the risk involved, consider a simple imaginary example from the field of automation.[31] Imagine that in some science-fiction world an air conditioner were equipped with a robot arm which allows it, among other things, to reach out and turn the control knobs of other air conditioners. If controlled by appropriate computing machinery this could have obvious advantages. Suppose for example that two such air conditioners found themselves operating side by side in the same room. Unless their two thermostats were set for the same temperature, one of them would be bound to end up running flat out in the cooling mode, with its neighbour running flat out heating. The two would then wear one another out, each struggling to achieve its own goal, because of the disparity between the goal-settings. Here then is a situation where it would be of advantage for at least one of these devices to use its robot arm to adjust the thermostat of the other into coincidence with its own. By this communicative action it would achieve a situation beneficial to both: each could settle down to carry only half a normal load, because they now have the same goal.

So far, so good. But now imagine what could happen if one air conditioner, instead of using its communicative powers to adjust priorities in other air conditioners, were to start playing about with its *own* thermostat. Now things could go badly wrong. It might randomly turn the knob so that it began running flat out heating, or flat out cooling, overloading itself and rapidly burning out. Even worse, we could imagine some feedback from the room temperature that made it turn its thermostat convulsively first higher and higher, then lower and lower alternately, in a succession of unstable spasms. In such a case the thing would become completely unreliable as an air conditioner; it would no longer be pursuing a goal of the sort for which it was designed.

This notion, that allowing a system to play about with its own controls can be damaging to its designed function, is one we can profitably carry over to the case of the human organism. The ability of the human organizing system to adjust its own priorities corresponds at the mechanical level to what at the personal level we would call 'having a will of one's own'. In this area of the human repertoire, some fixed standards are essential if the system is not to develop pathological conditions, of the sort illustrated by our air conditioner.

Of course lower animals too can shift their target-settings. They will give up eating or drinking, for example, in order to flee from a predator. But although lower animals do sometimes run amok, they are saved from the worst sorts of self-induced disaster by having only a limited range of their priorities open to their own adjustment. Their behaviour is much more strongly determined by the in-built norms and standards of their genetic make-up. With man's more sophisticated powers of self-adjustment, developed along with the game of interpersonal communication, he faces the possibility of so messing about with his goal settings as to lose his way, missing the main point and purpose of his creation. A self-centred train of thought, pursued far enough without check, can completely alter his goal settings from those that would make sense in terms of his Creator's design, so that he renders himself unfit for the role that alone gives him his truest dignity. Left to himself he becomes the restless creature sketched by so many of our modern novelists, chameleon-like, given to incoherent and pointless changes of style. Without adequate external landmarks and accepted constraints and the readiness to steer by those landmarks, his power to shape his own priorities becomes a curse, and his self-inflating efforts after dignity a pathetic offence to the moral universe. Moreover, just as with the air-conditioner, states of self-centred independence easily become self-reinforcing, by what the engineer calls 'positive feedback'. The sorts of sub-routine that give rise to behaviour we describe by words like envy, greed, brutality, slovenliness, selfishness, are particularly liable to become self-reinforcing and indeed self-protecting in this way. To put it in personal terms, our *pride* resists any interference with our power to set and modify our own priorities in these areas.

You may object that all this is only natural, and hardly surprising. Of course I agree. It is natural all right; but it can be none the less disastrous for our capacity to get to know God. By distorting and limiting our internal repertoire, it creates conceptual blind spots precisely in the area to which the Christian Gospel is directed; for it is especially in the area of our self-centred will and its pathology that God offers to make himself real in our human experience, by re-ordering our priorities in a way we cannot do for ourselves. Worse still, in this natural condition we are liable to self-reinforcing mis-perceptions of what the Gospel is all about. Just as a drug addict may misperceive those who try to help him as hostile, threatening, cruel, unfeeling and so forth, so our self-reinforcing grip on our own controls, natural though it is, can offer a deadly barrier to realistic communication. Our natural pride can make God's most loving and earnest appeals sound *meaningless* to us, if we insist on protecting the areas of our internal repertoire on which his message is designed to have its shaping function. Conversely, if we once begin to loosen our spasmodic grip, even if only by considering what it would mean for our priorities if we *were* convinced of the truth of Christ's claims, then more and more of what he has to say will come to have an increasingly clear meaning for us – whether we like it or not.

Atheistic Humanism

To some unbelievers the suggestion that a man's self-sufficiency and rebelliousness can act as a barrier to the knowledge of God is, in the words of H. J. Blackham, 'an insult, a violation of himself and his whole experience'. Blackham is perhaps typical of people who can be called 'humanist' in the sense that they stand, as Christianity does, for human fulfilment and for the importance of compassion and self-reliance; only they angrily reject what Christian humanism affirms, that the only true fulfilment is to be found in working out our destiny in line with the will of our Creator, through whom alone we can hope to learn what true compassion and healthy self-reliance mean. A generation ago people with atheistic views of this kind liked to call themselves 'scientific' humanists. There was more than a suggestion in this that they had scientific warrant for their rejection of Christian belief. Nowadays the cloud that has come over the reputation of science has made this term less popular; but the basic attitude remains common. It combines the assumption that science has made belief in God impossible with a bitter resentment of the deflation of human pride implicit in the Christian Gospel. According to H. J. Muller,[32] for example, in a collection of essays called *The Humanist Frame* published some years ago: 'Once the theory of evolution was accepted, only *wishful thinking* could avoid the *logical* conclusion that man has created God in his own image' (italics mine). Julian Huxley[33] echoes the same idea: 'In the evolutionary pattern of thought there is no longer either need or room for the supernatural . . . Evolutionary man can no longer take refuge from his loneliness by creeping for shelter into the arms of a divinized father-figure whom he has himself created.'

Once we move from negatives to positives, however, the atheist position is less distinctive. What do atheistic humanists do? 'Humanists,' says Muller, 'unequivocally face up to the world as it actually is, assess man's place in it, gauge the possibilities of the future, and plan realistically for their species.' This had better be equally true of Christian humanists! Indeed the positive beliefs of godless humanism, as stated by Julian Huxley,[34] are so unexceptionable as to verge on the banal: 'The central belief of evolutionary humanism is that *existence can be improved,* that vast *untapped possibilities can be increasingly realized,* that greater *fulfilment can replace frustration.*' Huxley goes on to suggest that 'a kind of religion could be based on the scientific view of man'. 'The emergent religion of the near future,' he says, 'could be a good thing. *It will believe in knowledge* (sic). Instead of worshipping supernatural rulers it will sanctify the higher manifestations of human nature in art and love, in intellectual comprehension, in aspiring adoration, and will emphasize the fuller realization of life's possibilities as a sacred trust.'

An innocent reader of such passages might be forgiven for concluding that Christianity does not stand for these positive things. But of course the truth is the reverse: that these writers are simply borrowing the ingredients they like in the Christian emphasis on the sacredness of truth and the infinite worth of human beings, and differing from the Christian chiefly in what they deny.[35] To claim as a 'logical conclusion' from evolutionary theory that 'man has created God in his own image' is itself a prize example of wishful thinking.

Humanists of this stripe object particularly to the idea that we have reason to be ashamed before God, and that we need his forgiveness for our resistance to his loving claims on our priorities. Of course it must be agreed that if Christianity were known to be false then in Blackham's words such talk would be 'an insult'. But to talk in these terms begs the question. For if, however unpalatable, the biblical diagnosis is the sober truth, would it not be more of an insult to our fellow men to make no effort to bring home to them these vitally important facts about themselves?

No one has more clearly expressed this point than the great Blaise Pascal, who was one of the seventeenth-century pioneers of modern science, and incidentally invented one of the first arithmetical computing machines. His famous *Pensées (Thoughts on Religion and Philosophy)*[36] contain some of the most penetrating analyses ever written of the predicament in which man lands himself by rejecting his Creator's authority over his priorities. 'The essence of self-love,' he says, 'is to love only oneself; to be interested for nothing but oneself. But what is gained by this? A man cannot prevent this object of his love from being full of defects and miseries; he wishes to be great, and sees himself to be little; he wishes to be happy, and feels himself miserable; he wishes to be perfect, and sees himself full of imperfections; he wishes to be an object of the esteem and love of his fellow men, and sees that his faults deserve their aversion and contempt. This embarrassment produces the most unjust and criminal passion imaginable; for he conceives a mortal hatred against that truth which forces him to behold and condemn his faults; he wishes it were annihilated, and unable to destroy it in its essence, he endeavours to destroy it to his own apprehension, and that of others; that is, he employs his utmost efforts to conceal his defects, both from himself and others, and cannot bear that men should point them out to him, or even see them. Certainly, to be full of defects is an evil; but it is a much greater evil, if we are full of them, to be unwilling to know the fact; since this is adding a voluntary illusion to their number . . . What a chimera, then, is man! what a novelty! what a chaos! what a compound of inconsistencies! A judge of all things, yet a feeble earthworm: a depository of truth, yet a heap of uncertainty: the glory and the outcast of the universe' (loc. cit. pp. 9, 10, 46).

Pascal's message, however, is fundamentally not one of despair but of hope – the marvellous hope that comes when we stop pretending to self-sufficiency and accept the humbling Truth that can heal us. For 'amongst other astonishing facts of the Christian religion this is one, that it reconciles man to himself in reconciling him to God.' 'Our self-will is never satisfied, even when it has obtained all it desires; but we are satisfied the instant we renounce it.' Reinhold Niebuhr[37] has more pungently expressed a related thought: 'Religion is not as is generally supposed an inherently virtuous quest for God; it is merely the final battleground between God and man's self-esteem.'

Palatable, or True?

No: the truth is that once you have seen through its 'nothing-buttery', the atheistic 'humanist' assault on Christianity derives any plausibility it has from a confusion of two questions that ought to be kept quite distinct: (a) is Christianity palatable? (b) is Christianity true? These people marshal ample negative evidence on the first question, and then allow their readers to assume that because Christianity is unpalatable to the natural heart it must be rejected as untrue. How many times in an argument about Christianity have you heard people say: 'but I wouldn't like to believe in a god like that'? Talk about wishful thinking! Can you imagine a scientist rejecting a colleague's findings by saying: 'But I wouldn't like to believe in an isotope (or whatever) like that'? To speak in such terms is simply not to take rationally or seriously the question whether in sober truth there is God to be reckoned with. If there is, then whether or not one wants him to exist is irrelevant. He has to be reckoned with as he is. If there isn't, our wants are equally irrelevant. The fact of the matter is that Christianity does not pretend to be palatable to our fallen human nature. But if its diagnosis is true, and if God's remedy is available, then it is clearly the best news that sick humanity could hear. Christians who have found God as good as his word from their own experience have every reason, as a matter of compassion, to urge that news on their fellow men as the truth that can heal them.

Man's truest dignity can be realized only by facing up to reality, whatever the cost: whether it be at the cost of his self-esteem or anything else. If we pre-define what that reality must be, in a spirit of self-sufficiency and proud rejection of any claims on our obedience by our Creator, we can block ourselves off from the one way in which we could discover what reality is about by coming to know its Giver. Conversely, if we will only allow that Giver to get under our self-esteem, to re-order our priorities, we will find our eyes being opened. We will come to realize the truth – indeed the sobering truth – of the biblical diagnosis of our condition, and the glorious truth of the remedy that God has made available through Christ to those who are ready to ask for it in realistic repentance. The New Testament is full of powerful statements of this theme. Here for example is Paul writing to the Romans: 'What return did you get from the things of which you are now ashamed? The end of those things is death. But now that you have been set free from sin and have become slaves of God, the return you get is sanctification and its end, eternal life. For the wages of sin is death' (that is the diagnosis), 'but the free gift of God is eternal life in Christ Jesus our Lord.'[38] Or as he puts it when writing to the Corinthians: 'If any one is in Christ he is a new creation; the old has passed away, behold, the new has come. All this is from God, who through Christ reconciled us to himself and gave us the ministry of reconciliation; that is, God was in Christ reconciling the world to himself, not counting their trespasses against them, and entrusting to us the message of reconciliation. So we are ambassadors for Christ, God making his appeal through us. We beseech you on behalf of Christ, be reconciled to God.'[39]

Why is this issue not more obvious to those outside the Christian Church today? Can anything be done to make it more clear and urgent to our fellow men? I believe that Harry Blamires,[40] in his book *The Christian Mind*, may have raised the key question for those of us who claim to be Christians. Is it possible that in our Christian thinking today, despite all our energetic evangelism, we are in danger of getting our priorities wrong? Is it true, as Blamires suggests, that the Christian mind is not sufficiently distinguishable from the secular mind? Are we Christian realists in all our thinking? Is eternity more important to us than time? Is God more precious than gold? These are questions that go deep. Our answers, the real answers we give in our hearts, will radically affect the kind of argument that we mount in defence of the dignity of man, as well as the kind of witness we bear to the truth of the faith.

What then is Special about Man?

What then is so special about man? What is so special about John Smith, about you or me? The biblical answer is that what makes us special is the amazing fact that our Creator was prepared to do for us all that Christ did and suffered in his incarnation, crucifixion and resurrection. Our dignity has nothing to do with our occupying a geographical hub of the universe, or being the product of a special process, or being constructed of special materials, or being inexplicable at one or another scientific level. We matter simply because he, our Creator, has conceived us in his own image so that he can address us, plead with us, rescue us, and forgive us. As such, rebellious though we are, he loves us with the love of a Father. If we only grasp what this means, it makes any self-satisfied posturing on our part unthinkable. Equally unthinkable would be any churlish rejection of the privilege he offers us. It is a false modesty that says: 'I am too humble to be interested in heaven or in eternal life.' If we recognize what our rescue has cost, we will not insult our rescuer by undervaluing the dignity to which we are called: the dignity of forgiven rebels, restored not as slaves but as sons, brothers of Christ, fellow heirs with him of his eternal Kingdom.

If we are biblically oriented, then, we will have no reason to make a theological fuss about questions of the scientific explicability of man, or the other scientific issues that we have looked at in these lectures. What is special about each man is the role to which he is called. We will be quick to distinguish dignity in this sense from *superiority,* whether measured psychologically, physically, or in any other way. We will be equally quick to see that true dignity has no stake in the myth of 'equality' that denies any differences between people's basic abilities; rather will we learn, and encourage our fellow men to learn, how to prevent our inequalities from harming our dignity. We will find no threat to our true dignity in our creaturely dependence on God. Above all, we will be realistic from the outset about what we must leave behind at the end of the day, remembering that only those priorities which are eternal can survive.

Perhaps this last point needs some expansion. As we have seen in earlier chapters, our personal identity is closely linked with our priorities. In a sense, what identifies me more fundamentally than anything else is my total 'goal-complex' or priority-scheme: what defines and orders all my aims and satisfactions in life, great and small. If I were to lose all of these, without replacement by others, I as a human personality would cease to exist. If that is the case, we do well to ask ourselves what it must mean for us, as individuals, that no priority incompatible with God's priorities can go with us into eternity. For if when we leave this life there are priorities we cannot take with us, this will be no merely incidental loss; for it is those priorities that in part *define who we are*. Throughout our lives, then, our greatest concern must be that those priorities of ours which are unfit for eternity should as quickly and completely as possible disappear from the goal-complex that defines who we are. If we cherish, as an essential part of what identifies us, priorities which are incompatible with God's eternal kingdom, then when God says that someone with such priorities cannot enter his kingdom he is not being arbitrarily intolerant. He is saying simply that since such priorities can have no existence in the new kingdom, nobody to whom these priorities are essential can exist in it either. If we want to be realistic in obedience to the biblical perspective on human nature and human dignity, then, our chief concern will be that while there is time God's grace may cause to atrophy in us all priorities and desires unfit for eternity, replacing them with better ones, in order that we can survive the transplantation without loss of identity.

The Need for Balance

My final plea is that we recognize the duty to be *balanced* in the emphasis that we give to *all* the facts about man, whether at the mechanistic, the psychological or the spiritual level. This is not only our duty to the God who gives us these facts, but also an essential feature of true respect for human dignity, which would scorn the suppression of any truth in its defence. Here again the biblical and the scientific traditions are at one in encouraging eagerness to do equal justice to all our data.

Pascal puts it well. 'I blame equally', he says, 'those who make it their sole business to extol man, and those who take on them to blame him, and those also who attempt to amuse him. I can approve none but those who examine his nature with sorrow and compassion . . . It is dangerous to show man in how many respects he resembles the lower animals, without pointing out his grandeur. It is also dangerous to direct his attention to his grandeur without keeping him aware of his degradation. It is still more dangerous to leave him ignorant of both; but to exhibit both to him will be most beneficial.' Again: 'How strange that Christianity should enjoin man to acknowledge himself worthless and even abominable, and at the same time to aim at resembling his Maker. Without the counterpoise which each of these injunctions forms to the other, his elevation would render him superlatively proud, or his abasement would render him dreadfully abject . . . No doctrine could be more suitable for man than that which informs him of this two-fold capability of receiving and losing grace, on account of the two extremes into which he is always in danger of falling, despair and pride' (loc. cit. pp. 6, 7, 79).

Seen in this light the human sciences, insofar as they are true to fact, are but allies of all who would help their fellow men to rise to their true dignity. They can readily be abused by enemies of human dignity in all three of Pascal's categories; but in principle I suggest that they have the same rich potential for good as all other of God's gifts, if received with thanksgiving and in 'the fear of the Lord', remembering that we who are responsible for using them are sinners too.

Let me end with an equally robust yet sensitive statement by an evangelical thinker of the present day, Dr. Bruce Milne:[41] 'The prodigal will not be returned to the homeland merely by shouting our traditional clichés from the security of the Father's house. We need to go to the far country and address him there, in the context of his self-understanding and experience. Our responsibility is not discharged by helping him to come to terms with the far country, or by convincing him that the swine husks are really an adequate diet for his empty aching belly. We have to make him see his situation in all its rebellious folly, yes to the point of his catching the stink of the pigsty in his nostrils; but we will speak too of the homeland, and delight to assure him of the sheer staggering miracle of a Father's mercy and all-forgiving grace, and of a renewed sonship and a new dignity and destiny in the family circle of God.'

Notes

Notes to Chapter 1

1. For an explanation of what is meant by 'embodiment', see Chapter 2.
2. Hooykaas, R: *Religion and the Rise of Modern Science,* Scottish Academic Press, Edinburgh, 1972.
3. Boyle, R: *The Christian Virtuoso,* 1906, in Boyle, *Works,* 5 vols., London, 1744, vol. 5.
4. Walter, J. A: Sociology & Religion – are they logically complementary? *Faith & Thought, 104,* 27–44, 1977.

Notes to Chapter 2

5. I have discussed this in more detail in *The Clockwork Image*, Inter-Varsity Press, London, 1974, and in *Science, Chance & Providence*, Oxford University Press, 1978.
6. Polanyi, M: *The Tacit Dimension,* Routledge & Kegan Paul, London, 1967, p. 40.

Notes to Chapter 3

7. Morris, D: *The Naked Ape*, McGraw-Hill, New York, 1968. Quotation by permission of McGraw-Hill Book Company. Published in UK by Jonathan Cape Ltd., London, 1967.
8. Dawkins, R: *The Selfish Gene*, © Oxford University Press, 1976. Quotations by permission of Oxford University Press.
9. Thorpe, W. H: *Animal Nature and Human Nature*, Methuen, London, 1974. See also his *Purpose in a World of Chance: A Biologist's View*, Oxford University Press, 1978.
10. Skinner, B. F: *Beyond Freedom and Dignity*, Jonathan Cape Ltd., London, 1972.
11. Jeeves, M. A: *Psychology & Christianity: the view both ways*, Inter-Varsity Press, London, 1976.
12. MacKay, D. M: *Freedom of Action in a Mechanistic Universe.* (Eddington Lecture), Cambridge University Press, London and New York, 1967. Reprinted in *Good Readings in Psychology* (M. S. Gazzaniga and E. P. Lovejoy, eds.), Prentice Hall, New York, pp. 121–38, 1971. See also note 5.
13. MacKay, D. M: Brain and Will. *The Listener*, May 9 and 16, 1957. Reprinted in *Body and Mind*, (G. N. A. Vesey, ed.), pp. 392–402, Allen and Unwin, 1964.

Notes to Chapter 4

14. The proceedings have now been published under the title of *Modifying Man: Implications & Ethics* (Craig W. Ellison, ed.), University Press of America, Washington, 1978. Quotations by permission of University Press of America.
15. Hook, Ernest B: 'Behavioral Implications of the Human XYY Genotype'. *Science, 179,* 139–50, 1973.
16. See his paper in reference 14.
17. Proverbs 22:6.
18. Sargent, W: *Battle for the Mind,* Greenwood, Westport, Connecticut, 1975.
19. Also in reference 14.
20. Genesis 19: 32–6.

Notes to Chapter 5

21. The theory of communication here outlined is discussed in more detail in my *Information, Mechanism & Meaning,* M.I.T. Press, Cambridge, Mass., 1969.
22. See Chapter 3, loc. cit. note 21.
23. *The Times,* Sept. 3, 1970, p. 9. © Times Newspapers Limited (London), 1970. Quoted by permission.
24. Philippians 4:8.
25. *The Times,* Aug. 3, 1976. © Times Newspapers Limited (London), 1976. Quoted by permission.
26. MacKay, D. M: Language, Meaning and God. *Philosophy, 47,* 1–17, 1972.
27. For examples, see R. A. Hinde (ed.) *Non-Verbal Communication,* Cambridge University Press, 1972.
28. Galatians 2:20.
29. 2 Corinthians 5: 20.

Notes to Chapter 6

30. Lorenz, K: *King Solomon's Ring,* Crowell, New York, and Methuen, London, 1952.
31. See Chapter 9 of ref. 21.
32. Huxley, J. (ed.), *The Humanist Frame,* Allen & Unwin, London, 1961, p. 402.
33. Huxley, loc. cit., pp. 18, 19.
34. Huxley, loc. cit., pp. 48, 26.
35. C. S. Lewis has a telling pen-picture of the bankruptcy of atheistic humanism in the characters of 'Sensible' and 'Humanist' in *The Pilgrim's Regress,* Geoffrey Bles, London, revised edition, 1943.
36. Pascal, B: *Thoughts on Religion and Philosophy,* translated by Isaac Taylor, John Grant, Edinburgh, 1894, pp. 9–10.

37. Niebuhr, R: *The Nature and Destiny of Man: Volume I. Human Nature*, Scribners, New York, 1941, p. 213. Quoted by permission.
38. Romans 6: 21–23.
39. 2 Corinthians 5: 17–20.
40. Blamires, H: *The Christian Mind,* S.P.C.K., London, 1963.
41. Milne, B: The Idea of Sin in Twentieth-Century Theology. *Tyndale Bulletin, 26,* 1975, p. 33. Quoted by permission.

Index